This DYING THING

THING

david payton

Order this book online at www.trafford.com
or email orders@trafford.com

Most Trafford titles are also available at major online book retailers.

Printed in the United States of America.

ISBN: 978-1-4669-4224-0 (sc)

Trafford rev. 06/06/2012

 www.trafford.com

North America & international
toll-free: 1 888 232 4444 (USA & Canada)
phone: 250 383 6864 ♦ fax: 812 355 4082

The COVER

On the cover is a picture of an upside-down dove. Death is sad to those who are left behind, and the person who died meant something to them. You know there are people who are glad people die. You must be aware that EVERYBODY has different views on death. Some are tragically attacked by it, and others think it's funny. Suicide is something else, too.

There are a cluster of birds flying over the dove. Maybe those birds are vultures. Have you ever taken man out of the picture and see how well the world functions without interference? Isn't it possible that ants and termites consume wood because when a tree dies it has to be disposed of, and you can rest assure, ants and termites have been around longer than housing.

A fence at the bottom with a single bird. Death can be lonely. Some people die of loneliness. Some die without friends or family.

There is also a nest and a bird on the word thing. For the most part, death only pauses us as a whole for a moment or two. The rest of the world goes on loving or killing. Mating or destroying. Laughing and Crying. Death only pauses us for a moment or two. The bulk of us go on plotting and stealing. Healing and helping. Investigating, or doing nothing. We can name the formation of stars, but we can't get along. We can see on Mars, but we can't get along. We can invent, and yes we are destructive. The perpetual flower of eternity. **This Dying Thing**. I don't think we will ever get a handle on it.

Written by
David Payton

Graphic Layout by
Lynn Tolliver, jr.

Set up and edited by
Pat Frances

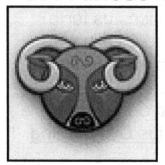

There are many contributing writers in this book. If you are looking at this book to check the grammar, or how it is written –

YOU ARE MISSING THE POINT

Pat Frances

The inspiration of this book came from the death of my mother, Frances Edith Nix – Tolliver. She died February 19th, in the early morning hours in Suburban Pavilion, which is a nursing home in Cleveland, Ohio. She was born April 24th, 1920, she would have been 87 this year, but I was not fortunate enough to have her that long, however I was fortunate enough to have her 56 years of my life. Some of this information will probably be repeated in the chapter, or chapters dedicated to her. I will try to, the best of my ability, order in chronological, deaths that have been significant in my life. I will probably repeat this, but we are not raised to die, we are raised to live, even though the plot from mankind is like they would do sheep, cow or chickens – although you are cared for to a certain degree, you are not going to make it out of this world alive. Just not. My thought on this is, that if we were raised to die, there would probably be more tragedy, probably be more destruction and chaos, and then again maybe not. I also agree that because there are enormous amounts of people, and quite a few that would like to run the world a certain way, we will never unite to a calm and peace that can exist given the right circumstances.

I will say this, too – I am fortunate enough to live the 56 years that I have, and see her die. I could have died when I was shot back in '86, the day after Christmas, but I was spared. I wouldn't have seen the granddaughter from my son, Orrin, and a lot of things. If you understand that statement, perhaps there is hope for you. Not knowing what tomorrow may bring, there it is, if you wake up and face it. There it is. Having the wisdom to appreciate, or not. Knowing what you need to know, to get to the next level in your life, but knowing all the time – we are not going to get out of here living in the flesh sense of the word. Not. And the question I ask now – if you were to die this very moment, did you do everything you wanted to do, that you could, or were you saving it for a moment in time that was not guaranteed to you? Don't answer that question, just get smarter. Not really knowing where we go when it's over, why not get the best out of what you are capable of getting, right now, here on earth?

When my father died, it had an effect on me, as many deaths have, but it inspired me to write this song several years after, because I have wrestled deaths of loved ones in my dreams. I was in Detroit, Michigan, half way playing my guitar and made a song up that a school chum sang with me on. He also went to the same church I did, when we were young kids.

His name is Gerald Shields. In fact, I used the G in his name to come up with GO music, but it was already taken, so it became OG, because my first name begins with an O. The song is called,

"When Someone Dies"

When Someone Dies, So Many Cry.
My World Is Black, They Don't Come Back.

In A Lifetime, Why Do We Do It?
Seeing Life's So Short. Ain't Nothing To It.
We Fuss And Fight, Don't We Know?
That Before Too Long, We All Must Go
To A Place That's Far Away. It's In White & Black.
When We Go, We're Gone To Stay, And We Don't Come Back.

When Someone Dies, So Many Cry.
My World Is Black, They Don't Come Back.

You Listen Close To Me, My Words Are True
All The Agony And Grief, When Someone Dies On You
I Can Tell, Almost Feel, It's The Very End.
You Don't Know How, And Won't Know When!
When Someone Dies, You Feel So Sad
And If You Loved Them So, It Hurts So Bad.

When Someone Dies, So Many Cry
All My World Is Black, When They Die They Don't Come Back.

Before I get going, I want to express a couple of additional things. Please understand, this book is how I see it, I can't make a statement that this will be filled with facts. There will be theories, and life in my eyes, concepts, whatever. Through our lives, will we ever really know what the truth is about things, and if we find out, if we tell people, will they understand?

I don't think any man or woman can walk the face of the earth and experience everything, or do everything. There are people who have lived the maximum and have probably barely scratched 5% of what could have been accomplished, if their lives had been planned perfectly. So many things you think about, so many things you can do, so many things you don't, for whatever reason.

There have been experiments that have taken place, so the history books have told us. Pierre and Madame Marie Curie did a process on death. Look it up, if you're interested. I'm sure a lot of people have had scientific views of the dead. It is surely a mystery.

Here are my thoughts. The dead don't hate. The dead can make the living hate, but the dead don't hate. I don't think the dead can kill, or do anything to you. The belief of the dead can create other things, but have we ever been given actual proof that the dead can do anything, but be where they are, off this planet? I think our believing is the only thing that keeps those who have departed alive.

What about this theory. What if there is an afterlife, and it is so beautiful as we are told, and if the dead have a chance to come back, let's say, if someone died and went to this haven of glory and said – "I bet if I go back and tell people how it is here, they will change their ways." And those in charge tell them, you can go back, but you won't go back as whom you died as, and you won't know anybody that you knew when you were alive. And you have to start all over again through the baby phase. And you are given that option.

Or this. Think about this because I have a very vivid imagination it sometimes scares me. What if someone who is unconscious, or someone who has changed their complete personality is actually someone who died and came back during the time that person was going through their change. This would give the new back-from-the-dead person a chance to learn all they needed to know, but the person is a new inside.

Has anyone ever acted or seemed to be different and you asked them or said –

"You don't act the same, are you okay?"

"Everything okay? There's something different about you."

"Since so&so has come back, they act different."

I believe there are many things we will never have the answer to, ever. I believe there are many items in our life that will remain a mystery. The controversy of Ape's Evolution versus Adam Eve, the jury is still out is it not? How can we function without knowing the truth, and why are we allowed to have several theories on man. Is it possible the two co-exist? And I will say this again – I don't ever see any apes changing to man today. I don't see ANYTHING changing to anything. It is fact that there are things that use to be, that are no longer here. Life that has become extinct, but I don't see anything converting – DO YOU?

There have been movies made about death and the afterlife. I'm sure there has been a movie about Madam and Pierre Curie – but the one that stands out to me that probably wasn't really for entertainment was a movie called – BEYOND AND BACK.

The movie was released in 1978, and when I attended the movie so I could talk about it on the radio, most of the audience was older than I am now. They had to be in their 60s and 70s. It's listed as a docudrama. This means taken from documents, but dramatically produced for entertainment purposes.

Just briefly, the story was a series of people who were near death; they all saw a bright light and had similar experiences. Some were able to hover over their physical bodies in some kind of spirit form, but later returned.

Let me say this. I am not going to say I believe it or not believe it. I will be the first person to tell you, I don't have all the answers to everything, although a lot of people think I think I do, but I don't. It is very easy for me to tell you I don't know, and not to criticize you for what you believe in.

In Yoga, people have reported having out of body experiences. Don't look to me for credibility. I don't know. BEYOND AND BACK is narrated by Brad Crandall. He gave the movie a lot of authority, by the way he sounded. But let me say this to you – just because something sounds good, does not mean it is good. You can't judge a book by its cover works both ways. I think most people only look at something looking bad, and it turns out to be good, or someone looking poor or unworthy, turning out to be a class act or someone with character.

It works the other way, too.

Some people who look good, some people that have class, turn out to be thieves and con-artists. For appearance sake, hell is not going to look like hell, if they are working a mark. You have to be careful.

Because the movie looked the way it did, it appeared very credible, and probably offered "peace" for those who felt they didn't have much time left.

thoughts....
reality....
love....
happiness....

life –

isn't is something to behold?

Have you ever gone to sleep, and didn't dream, it was dark, totally. And then you woke up? What if death is that? That darkness, when you don't dream. Or what if death is a continuous dream? A series of nightmares, or a series of dreams patched together where you never awaken, yet you are still in the mindset of existence.

It's true; everything is not the same with everyone. What if there are several places that a dead can go, not just one or two. What if areas in that glorious haven, like there are continents here on earth? Who is to say what death is really like with proof? One thing for certain, dead people do not come back, or do they and not only we don't know, but they don't know?

What about people who have incurable amnesia? Is it possible one of those dead theories I mentioned earlier is where souls have been swapped? A soul that didn't have a decent shot in its previous life, gets traded out with the person's soul who has left the body because that soul's time was up. I know these may appear as ridiculous assumptions, but do you know for sure?

What about that feeling that you've seen someone some place before, and they say the same thing about you, but you can't remember. Is it possible that you are looking at each other's soul and you were together with that person in a previous existence? See what I mean about that imagination of mine?

At my mother's funeral – I saw a cousin from Detroit who looked just like my father. Just like him, more than I did. And there was someone who looked identical to my mother when she was younger. If I were to take a picture of the two of them standing together, they would probably look like my parents did. That was something.

What if that "familiar" face was your brother previously, and that is what you are looking at, and you were that person's brother too. Two brothers that were here before, and for some strange reason, the souls connect.

With all the traveling that we do, and all the people that we see, is it possible that some of those people that we never see again, were souls in bodies that have come back? Even though you have a fantastic conversation with them, or good time, you will never see that person again. Even though there was a level of comfort, and sometimes for some of us, excitement. Who can explain what that is? All the people that we see, but we never really meet them.

And what about people who attend funerals, that you don't know, but they are there? What is the meaning of that? Why would you want to go to a funeral of a person that you don't know?

Don't get me wrong about my imagination. Even though you may have never heard any of these summaries from anyone else, there are probably other people thinking about this very same thing.

Everybody is not capable of dealing with death the same way. As my mother told me when my father died, I said to her she had practice with people dying. She replied to me, "No, each one is different." That holds true for me, too, but that may not be the case for everybody.

Some people are on the machine, being kept alive assisted. Some people want to unplug, and others want the person to linger on with hope of recovery. Some people wish people in their life die, and even help by trying to murder them. Death comes in different shapes and sizes, different ways. Death is a spectrum.

Death is going to happen to all of us.

The question is –

Will you be ready, when it comes for you?

It's Saturday, March 03, 2007. There was a show on Verizon cable titled, Purgatory. It's about people who were killed, probably in crime. When I first saw this movie years ago, it was like a magical thing. For sure we have not experienced anything like this on earth, not to my knowledge – or have we? There are so many wonders on this planet yet to be discovered.

The town is called Refuge. The setting was a western setting. I love westerns. Except for the real tame western movies or programs, somebody dies. Here people had been shot, hung or stabbed. They kept the marks on their bodies, probably as a reminder of what they did, and how they died.

Looking up Purgatory in the dictionary, it says that –

' a condition or place in which souls of those dying penitent are purified from venial sins. ' Like a holding premise for a duration or period. I am not clear on that, so if you really want to know about it, you will have to research for yourself.

I could go on talking about movies, but I won't, I will only bring up a couple more, but you can search the web, or go to a movie rental place and check out all the movies that deal with dying, or have dying in it.

The second movie that followed Purgatory, was Legends Of The Fall. A brother was killed in the service, and the wife of a brother was ruthlessly killed because of a power struggle. The pain of death that circled the characters was touching, and emotional.

The last movie I will mention, will be Flatliners. This is where the cast allowed themselves to expire, to be brought back by the rest of the ones who were in on the experiment. They wanted to know what it was like to be dead, then come back and talk about it. That is probably a fantasy for many. Seeking the unknown, getting the answer – And what about the vampire perceptual, where sometimes the bite allows you to live forever. This Dying Thing. This Dying Thing. This Dying Thing.

this Dying thing

Letters To My Mother

MA –

I hope the other letter made you smile. You never told me about old age. Getting old is tough. Worse than raising kids.

I miss McKinley, but I know if I live long enough, he will know me again, and we will be together. But these are the prayers I have, so you know I still have faith in God. He has shown me some things.

I pray that if he has to take anyone of the four of me, Orrin III, David Christopher & McKinley, that he take me, and I pray that I would rather have him with his mother and LIVE, than to come be with me and die. I hope you understand that. I want my sons to be healthy and happy. I think about you every single day, and I have been blessed that I had you for a mother and my father was my father. I couldn't have asked for a better pair. I mean apple. I mean peach, you know what I mean. I tell people this,
There is no woman before, now or in the future that would have been a better mother than you, and the same for my father, and I mean that. I wish things were different, but I know God has plans.

You know that record I recorded a long time ago? People have recorded that song over and over, and you thought it was junk. You were right, but it was some pretty good junk. Are you smiling mommy?

Your wayward son –

ORRIN Jr.

Mother –

Right now, I'm a little sick. I have a sinus infection, but I'm sure I'll survive. I think about you every day. I'm sorry I can't see you, but I tell everybody the reason I have been able to hold on as long as I can is because you were my theory.

I love you with all of my heart and wish things could be different. But you never know what life has in store for you. I hope you are still alive when I am back on top. There are many good things that are going to happen, if I can remain alive.

Thank you for the love you gave me and you never left me, although I gave you many reasons to.

Your son –

Arrin (cause that's how you pronounced it.) Although you know my name is ORRIN.

Love you, MA.

other DEATH Situations

OTHER DYING SITUATIONS

More than several plus years ago, while experiencing carbon monoxide invasion in my home with my two older sons, the birds that we had in the basement kept dying. This made me think that carbon monoxide was and has been a threat for many years, and because as it was explained to me, birds have a low tolerance for carbon monoxide, which is why you shouldn't blow your breath at them (it was told to me, I don't know how legitimate that is), but if what I experienced was accurate, it seemed to be logical. Persons from yester decade probably had birds to safeguard against carbon monoxide threats. It's one of the silent killers in our life.

When I went to the pet shop to tell one of the managers about it, his reply was, "Pets die." That was an unfair response, because, the many birds that I had purchased, they shouldn't have died that soon, but they did.

But the truth of the matter is, not only do pets die, everything dies. Everything. The pet shop manager, probably just didn't want to reimburse me for my purchase, or be responsible to pay others for the death of a pet, even though it was soon. We were fortunate enough to get out of the house, because the level of CO two was better than two times the amount it was supposed to be, and the culprit was an old and faulty furnace, which was replaced.

Very often, the death of a pet, a companion pet, carries the same weight as a human death. Unless a pet goes mad, that pet probably remains more loyal, if you need that, than any human can ever try to become. And even though that topic is another book by another author, because I'm not a big pet person, why is that? Why is it that an animal can remain loyal to its master? And we the more intelligent, the more "civilized" cannot?

From the song "Mr. Bojangles" – "the dog upped and died, but after 20 years he still grieved." Death will probably go on to be, one of the unsolved mysteries, regardless of how advanced we become.

DEATH OF A JOB

While watching The ShawShank Redemption, which starred Tim Robbins & Morgan Freeman, there was a character played by James Whitmore who had apparently been in prison a numerous amount of years. Upon his release, after a small time, he hung himself. From what I gathered in the film, he had become accustomed to his routine in jail, that when he was released, he was no longer comfortable in his new environment, so it had saddened him to the point of suicide. That wasn't the crux of the picture, so the reason I didn't mention this in the suicide chapter – my bringing this up here is to say, that often our pattern of existence becomes more important than life, and means more than the surface purpose of what it appears to others.

I haven't taken a survey, but I think most of us work so we can afford to live and provide for ourselves and our family. I am going to take a long shot by saying, I think more than half of the work force would be happier in a different occupation that what they are working as now.

This is the employee I am talking about. The person who has a job that is the most important to them. Not because of their occupation, but because their job has become a way of life. If they were not able to go to work and interact with the people around them, it would kill them. And those groups of people in that circle, probably don't even know how important they are to that person, or people like this. And further, the person may not be working for compensation, but for the little comradely activity they exchange while working. They look forward to going to work, look forward the meetings, the company outings, look forward to all of the activity that occurs, because of their job. Their job has become the reason they exist.

Because you see the people around you, every day consistently, it's possible you can establish a stronger relationship with people you work with, than family, or a friend.

Companionship at work can be bonded thicker than family or friend, because the interaction can be without emotion, expectation or restriction.

At the job, you are around people, speaking, having lunch, taking breaks together – sometimes you take breaks at the same time, you don't even speak to each other, yet you are together. In work areas – the communication, think of the assorted situations that become systematical. Employers that have cafeterias within them, the large corporations that could be a small town; and the employees are a part of this operation, functioning daily.

And now, due to downsizing, new ownership, strategic retirement, position elimination, you are out of a job. Something you did for 5 years, maybe even 30 years, like clockwork. You've been removed from a daily you had got use to, and again, not because you needed the money, you needed this behavior because it fulfilled purpose and the needed camaraderie that didn't exist in your life through friends or a family. This job death can be disabling, mentally depressing. And although not life terminating – still a major impact to a person's soul.

There are so many things that have an effect on a person, millions, which never get uncovered. The forward motion of progress moves, leaving many souls on the side of the road of torment and misery, never reaching a resolution.

death can be sad

DEATH OF A LOVE RELATIONSHIP

When someone you love, dies, they are gone permanently from this earth. And if you've read this once or twice, or skipped around, or even have had a conversation with me, you'll know that I don't know what happens when someone dies. But there have been many times I've seen a couple live together in harmony for years, and then one of the partners die, and leave that grief and sorrow behind – or there is the case where a person meets someone and falls in love with them, and before they get a good start, one of the two-in-love, vanish. Sometimes that person left behind, never really gets over that loss.

This 'death' of a relationship is not really where someone dies; it's where the love in that union starts to diminish. It's great when it diminishes on both of the parties' part, but when it dies in one of the people involved; the other is left to go on aching. How do you deal with a death like that? You've starting saving for a home, or you're living together. You meet relatives and get involved with each other's friends – then one day, (and probably not one day, something happens that irritates the other, or people find other people, or they just fall out), BAM! It hits you like a heavyweight prize fighter, and from the blind side, although sometimes you can tell, the bomb is about to drop, because the interest changes.

How do you function if you thought 'he' or 'she' was the one, and now they've moved on? Was that the way it was supposed to be? Then every person that you meet for a while after that is compared to the one you can't get out of your system, but they have chunked you out of their heart, out of they life, just out.

You had songs together – you went to that restaurant, or bar. You had a favorite movie. Think of how many people that can be in that situation. Very often, children are involved, yet that significant other is going 80 mph in a 20mph zone, with no stop sign ahead, while you remain parked. The death of a passion place, the end of ritual of romance – gone, with no recourse but to hurt. Maybe for the rest of your life. It probably would have been better if that person had died – did you ever think of that?

DEATH OF A FRIENDSHIP

A comic once told an audience, you can't blame a person for the way that person's family acted, or what they said or did. He then went on to say, you can pick your FRIENDS, but you can't pick your family. And you can't correct me on this one, but so many times a friend relationship can be closer than 'blood', in how they act and react with you. Outside of the actual dying of one, the death of a friendship can be very devastating, depending upon the depth of that union.

Most often, true friendship has nothing to do with a sexual or physical encountering. It is the true meeting of the minds, no holds barred, everything matters and total acceptance of one, regardless of their shortcomings – and hear me on this one, in some circumstances, FAMILY can be FRIENDS, and that has to be the most closest – the most tragic when that connection is disconnected.

You tell your friends things you won't tell anyone. As a person involved in a marriage or love affair, you won't tell your sig-other things that are right or wrong within that pairing, but you will tell a friend. Your friends may learn to know more things about you than anyone, and there sometimes exists a level of trust beyond trust.

When you lose your job, or you break up with a partner. When your parents are harassing you, and they don't listen, your friends do. It's like group therapy, and, you don't always have to tell your friends when you're on the outs, they sense it, and respond, telling you, when you feel like talking, talk, if not, we'll still be there for you, and you feel better – knowing that you have a comfort level that you can run to. If your children are giving you problems and you can't figure a turning point.

I will be the first to say, like a phone company said in a yesterday-century advertisement, a phone call is the next best thing to being there. For some, that works – but you can't go bowling over the phone. If you have a friend that has children the same age or the same interest as yours, and they become best friends, you can't do that over the phone.

There are so many combinations of friendship – from the full blown friendship, living the everyday, to just passing by the same people that begin to recognize you and wave as you go by each time, never to ever actually talk to them – but you have this kindred thing, where, even though you don't know what kind of person each of you are, you slightly know them and become familiar and use to seeing each other each morning, or whenever you see them, that you begin to 'miss' them when they've stop.

I had a neighbor like that, that lived across the street from me. His name was Jim. He would sit on his porch everyday, and speak to me. We were different ethnically, but we became 'distant friends'.

Too many different scenarios to list them all, but any of you reading this can think of the variety of connects that have brought benefit to one's self worth and enjoyment, so there are many ways those relationships can terminate.

There is the jealous friend, who thinks you spend too much time with another friend, when they thought you and "they" should have been closer. Or friends that got together because they both had nothing of value, but when one obtained that 'worth', the goodness that they shared with you became cheap. And not a word goodbye, or an explanation why, they pull the vanishing act, and you thought you had something. That friendship, suffered a death.

Or what if you're friends with your family, a sibling, parent or child and that new love in your life feels threatened of that relationship you have with your fam, and finds a way to finagle you away from your friendly-family – and the odd part is, your fam would have taken your new beau (or bonnet) with open arms, because it was you – but instead, termination of a very valuable.

You've spent time building this friendship. Friends that you can abandon for a while for whatever and when you resume contact, you are back on track – they know you and you know them. So close that if you say, "I Can't Talk Right Now", they don't question, they just wait, and perhaps even never request or expect a reason, they go on accepting you. Those are the friendships that are the tragic episodes when they die.

You lost your father or mother, and now this older person at work becomes or fills that void in your life, because their vision, the way they think has been beneficial for you, in fact that benefit has provided value to both of you, and now for whatever incident, that relationship is dead.

Except for the physical, and maybe even including that, a friend relationship can be one of the most life propelling things for you, and it is lost. Now you get sicker, now you are sadder, now you can't really deal with life's tragic blows, because that bond you had is Casper. (You know, *The Friendly Ghost* – in other words gone!) Some of you may not know who Casper The Friendly Ghost is – look it up on the Internet.

Have we been raised to die? Have we been prepared when a loved one leaves and it's only one-way, not mutual? Have we been taught how to survive the death of a friendly relationship? I don't think we have. Maybe there ought to be classes in school called **HOW TO DEAL**. All of us are not going to be lawyers or dentists. Only a small selection of us will be teachers – Farmers aren't everywhere and computer experts – BUT ALL OF US NEED TO KNOW....

HOW TO DEAL with this, what ever your THIS is.

media
Deaths
Media Deaths

MEDIA DEATHS

For as long as I can remember, there have been NEWS FLASHES, BULLETINS, BREAKING NEWS, and these THIS JUST INs in the broadcasting and journalism world. How we respond to different people who died and why they died has been amazing to me. Based on how a person is rated, determines the interest of that person's death. But in the true meaning of caring and sympathy, I don't think anyone should get a higher rating than the next when it comes to a death score, but that's just me.

The obituary section is a very popular section in all the newspapers across the country. I use to say when I was on the radio strong, "Check the obituary section in the paper – if your name is not on it – you're alive!" And then I would go into a spill on how to be grateful and what you can do, *if you want to do it.*

Who died today? And although we skim around the subject and chirp briefly on the topic, as a world, we are not really ready to deal with death, as important as it is to the survival of the world.

This section is not categorized in any fashion, not alphabetically, or with any rhyme or reason, just a handful of the fairly well know deaths that have happened, that spanked the headlines. And as a foot note, I hope this book is helping you deal with any tragedy that you have gone through, or go through.

DR. DEATH: Jack Kevorkian

Not very popular now, but back in the 90s or so, Jack Kevorkian assisted people who wanted to die for whatever reason. I think he even did some prison time, because it was quite controversial, although the family members of the deceased were heavily in favor of Jack Kevorkian removing the pain from the person who succumbed to his machine, and the members of the family who suffered.

During the emerging of Dr. Death – it reminded me of the movie, SOYLENT GREEN, which starred Edward G Robinson, and Charleston Heston, the actor pro-gun guy. Edward G had grown tired of his life, as I'm telling the story and decided to check out on his own in this huge facility. And it was probably legal in the movie, because all the taxes and profits and regulations were on point – but I believe eventually, it will be accepted here, in the real world.

Ed G was able to pick the music he wanted to hear, the colors he saw his last moments, the total atmosphere. It's this choice you have to go, while you're in your sane self, that may be the best way to go – if you're tired, and you have that legal option. So let me ask you this, if you don't mind – If you had a chance to pick how you were going to die, would you prefer an auto accident, or Jack Kevorkian? Would you like to drown or Jack Kevorkian – and not in the pain mode, but in a solid state of mind?

I think if assisted suicide was legal, the death rate would soar. I see a lot of sad faces, where it looks like people are only existing, not living. But let me go on to say, I'm not God. I was in a situation recently with discussion of a family matter, and I could not pull the plug – but I'm sure there are a lot of people who can and will – a lot of people who would pull the plug on themselves, depending how depressed or sad they were, or if they wanted to get back at somebody, sort of having the last word, even though it's a silent one.

If you are unhappy with your life, you need change. Change where you live - change where you work - change your romantic relationship, OR change the way you think. If you don't change, your life won't change and you will remain unhappy. If you CAN'T change, you will have to accept it, and be happy with that.

Randorri

JOHN LENNON

Lennon was part of one of the most popular music groups in the history of music. I was a huge Beatles fan, back in the time period they existed. The British Invasion was what it was called. Isn't it amazing that the first British invasion was during the Paul Revere days, and the Boston Tea Party, because that British invasion was a negative to Americans, but this British invasion was a musical delight and surprise? I'm sure there were many jealous American musicians, but we won't hear those stories, no.

John Lennon, probably the most intelligent Beatle, was shot just outside of his New York apartment. Who shot him and why is not the thrust of this section of the book, but the fact of his death. The things he did during his time of reign are mild now, compared to what some of the performers are pulling off today.

One of the things that stood out to me was, now silent, Rick James who was a Black artist, took a hit in his heart when he heard that John Lennon had been killed. What media does is, when a celebrity takes a hit like that, they get the comments of other people in the public eye, to get a bearing on how it may affect all of us. I said to myself, Rick James was bothered by that? Wow. From the things I heard about Rick James, I didn't think anything would matter to him, but sex and song, and probably in that order, but there it was, Rick James had been stunned.

John Lennon, the word man. He probably helped bridge some of the world together with his partners and their music. To me, they seemed to be one of the closest groups in my sight, like Booker T. & The MGs. There seemed to be some kind of magic glue, which held them all together. I was in Detroit at the time it happened, and although that seemed to mean a lot to everyone at the time, look how many murders have happened since then, and no stopping in sight – ever. So what does it really mean? And... what does that tell you?

NATALEE HOLLOWAY

The young teen that was swept away in Aruba. I followed the story, because it was everywhere in the news. It's tough to beat the home team, because they are playing on their turf. There are cracks and crevices that we'll never be able to find in Aruba, because there are cracks and crevices here in the states we don't know about. There are cracks and crevices in our minds we don't know about.

Here's where the problem lies in our coming closer to putting stolen youth killings to an end – because we all are not hurting at the same time – our concerns and efforts have little strength. If two million teenage daughters go missing simultaneously, I'm sure there would be stronger motions to bring this to a head. We're guarding cigars and fruit – when we should be watching life instead.

Natalee Holloway was an example of how this can happen to anybody. There are no restrictions. Her parents had been divorced I guess, and I can even go as far to guess again, I bet one of them didn't want her to go to Aruba. You can get drunk here in Colorado, or Texas. You don't have to go out of the country for that. You can party hearty in Michigan, or New York, you don't have to travel across the waters for a good time.

I've seen misery. How do you really get past the pain of losing a child? I know as a parent, I wish I could just wrap my arms around my little ones and protect them from all harm. Be there for every moment danger is abounding, but you can't. All the words of caution, the earning of trusts, and teachings of how to be careful, and it didn't stop anything.

And from our exterior looking interior – Natalee looked like a fair enough young lady. She appeared to be on the right track. To prevent this from continuing, how do we create a safe atmosphere for children, young adults to have the wild times they desire, but the danger-free zone reign to play in? Natalee Holloway is gone forever, and her parents are still here to drown in their memories. What tragedies we must endure, and painfully, never forget.

BARRY WHITE, THE MAESTRO

In the music industry, there were two guys that came on the scene at the same time, with big, big voices. One was Isaac Hayes, who at the time of this writing, still alive – and Barry White. Both had strong appeal for either of the sexes, the man or the woman. Isaac Hayes, for the ladies, because he was softer and mellow, but his outside exterior was aggressive and manly, so that appealed to the guy.

Barry White on the other hand, appealed to the women, and contraire to the physical look that Hayes had, Barry was a chubster. He had curls, but was a lot more professional in his look than sir Isaac. From what I have heard, they say to heavier people, if you want to look your best, dress as nice as you can. That's suppose to take away from the weight, you also have on.

Barry hit the music scene, hard. He had a female group, an orchestra and his solo career. I started hearing him do commercials for food. I was impressed with him reaching that plateau, but a lot of people had been wooed by the charisma of The Maestro.

I saw him in concert once. He had a full orchestra behind him, just like on his records. I thought to myself, that traveling bill had to be phenomenal, but someone told me – he didn't travel with a complete orchestra – he had a little combo, and hired the local orchestra in each city that he went to.

I remember him calling me, out of the blue – after starting to play his song, "Sho You Right", which was on A&M records at the time and just said to me. "You started playing my song in heavy rotation? Man, anything you want – anything." In that deep Barry White voice. The fact that he called me was different, not because he was Barry White, but because people out of your reach, usually don't reach out. I never called him, but I appreciated his.

When I heard he was sick, I figured it would be a matter of time before he wouldn't be around anymore, but from his songs, I'm sure many a family got a kick start. He shall be remembered in his song. There are a lot of them for all of us to cherish.

MARTIN LUTHER KING JR.

What did the death of Martin Luther King, Jr. mean to me? It didn't mean anything to me at the time. I really didn't know him, or really know about him. And this is not to lessen his value with the contributions his life meant, and what his death means, even to this day – I'm not saying that. I was angry because of him and not because he was assassinated. I was angry because my father made me stay home from school that day. I had perfect attendance! Check my records – I was a young teen, and was shock-treated to get good greats, have a great attitude and go to school everyday.

I had good grades; I was on the National Junior Honor Society, making the honor role and the merit role, with the greatest citizenship. (What a hook they had in our mouths!) We were fish for the catching, yes- we were gullible. I was going for the triple-double, with perfect attendance, and now this.

Judging by some of the things I've seen in life, I don't think Blacks claim the past for the benefit of the progress of their people. I call it the calculator theory – you get the answer without the logic. I personally think the Jewish nation uses the pain of their past for the fairway to their future. They don't forget, so you'll always remember, and hold that plateau of living standard, so you won't buckle during the on slaughter.

I didn't know who Martin Luther King Jr. was and I'm ruining my perfect attendance for him. Didn't make any sense. I'm not blaming my parents – life tosses you obstacles and demolition courses to sidetrack you from the prize. And the bulk of the percentage of all of us falls for that. We are all cows, getting whipped and pronged into the direction the forces want us to go into – the reason for the entire calamity we duration.

I was angry at Martin Luther King Jr., angry. I didn't get it. For what purpose? I wasn't taught to try for perfect attendance, UNLESS,...... it was, <u>try for perfect attendance</u>. I was almost at the finish line – and Martin Luther King Jr. made someone in my relay drop the ball. It was like stacking those items to balance, and you are almost finished and your project falls to pieces. That may have been the turning point in my trying to achieve – those mix signals you get. Tell you one thing, but forget to emphasize, but not if. Do what I tell you, not what you see me do. Follow my instructions, but use your own judgment – there are bound to be mistakes, and then not really an explanation on the punishment, or the now new way you're to do something – just keep up. Some of us need a manual on how to put this life thing together. Sorry kids! – All sold out!

At this older age, I know what the hoopla was all about. The big difference Martin Luther made for the complete nation, and perhaps the world. The difference that John F. Kennedy made. There are many, I can say a lot of celebrity deaths that have happened. Political figurines, which will hold a marker in the history writings forever. More than a handful murdered, which is a contrast to dying from an illness, or an accident. Martin Luther King Jr. was intentionally murdered.

But that didn't matter to me at that time. I was clueless to his value. It was just another guy that really didn't exist to me. And I don't feel bad about how wrong I was at the time, that's just the way some people look at a person's death and importance, *if they don't know.* And let me close this part by saying – that is also the way people who may know feel – they just may not tell you or show you – or depending upon their character – they just might – you may be just too blind to see it.

THE SMITH BOYS

In 2001, Andrea Pia Yates drowned her five sons. To this day, I still don't see why people, who are tired of their children, don't give them up for adoption, or try to get a relative to take care of them. Believe me I know that a lot of people kill others and even themselves to get at someone, and I understand there is a reason for everything, although people say there isn't a reason – there is. We may not understand the reason, we may not LIKE the reason, but there is a reason – even if that reason is no reason. Worrying about WHY, doesn't stop anything – we waste a lot of time figuring out why, when we should try to walk toward that preventive mode. We can't treat life, like we treat colds. We attack the symptoms – the virus is still there. We've only addressed the problem cosmetically. To see footage of the five boys and then to hear that they were dead from their mother's hand in the matter – wicked. And although the country was aware of this incident, how many of us are thinking about it now? Not to make light of this, but, there are other things, a cake in the oven, didn't bring those schematics home from the plant, other things that rush back into our lives, after a mini-mass horrible murder.

What made the killing of the two, a little more media driven than the killing of five, was the mother who allowed her two little precious gems to ride to their death in a car into the lake, was she lied about it, blamed an African American (a Black person), stirred up some drama and a bucket load of tears. Probably a small lakeful of eye precipitation. That mother of five, admitted to, did not charade us – that mother of two had the whole world looking for those two boys, knowing all along she had taken the lives of her own babies.

The deaths of babies, although no different in the score of getting killed on the meter of appeal has little weight, sometimes I wonder if, that had been my mother, and she let me and my sister take that finale trip, I would not be alive today. Although evil is raising its ugly head to show the world all the horrendous, hideous, repulsive activity that goes on in the world, we are also getting appreciation for the fact, we did not have to go through that, and be grateful for your life, regardless of how depressing you think it is. And it may be depressing – but take a good look around you – there are many in the world putting up with worse, BIG TIME.

When the news came on about the two boys missing, then later discovering they had been murdered by their mother – what were those little angels thinking as they were going into the water, WITHOUT THEIR MOTHER? How long did the mother think about this, and what was her real reason? They had a father who would have gladly taken them.

Do we think about all the other people involved, not just the immediate parents? What about the grandparents, or the uncles and aunts? What about the cousins – What about the people who want children and can't have them and here are people who can have them and are getting rid of them, dreadfully?

At the time this happened, my sons were young, I have a young son now – What could I be going through, that would make me want to try to hurt them, to get back at somebody, or if I think the world is not a good place for them to try to survive? Who gave me the authority to make that decision? **I credit my mother and father for raising me the right way, saying and doing the right thing, regardless of what they thought about individually**.

Although the mind is incredible for all it has to offer for the good. There are minds out there capable of anything. And this. Now that, just those seven are no longer here with us on earth, do their mothers smile any? Do they laugh any? Are they eating, and talking to other people? Do they get to go to the bathroom, on clean and presentable facilities? Has someone offered to marry them?

The greatest theft – the taking of a life. Children killing their parents, and parents killing their children. And here's the kicker for you – this has been happening for a long time. We just don't hear about all of them.

take
time out
for
yourself

DON HARRISON / CNN HEADLINE NEWS

I was an avid watcher of Headline News. As a radio broadcaster, you have to have an inkling of what's going on around you, if you want to have the perception of having some kind of knowledge. The big boys and girls will think you're just a joke, if you can't comment on a newsworthy topic, so my source of information came from Headline News. That would be one of the first things I did when I woke up to do mornings at WZAK.

In the beginning, 24 hours a day, around the clock, you could hear the whole capsule of the world in thirty minutes – sports scores, hot gadgets, everything. There were several at the time, Gordon Graham, Lynn Vaughn and Don Harrison. I thought it outstanding that Blacks (African Americans to some of you), were on this national network. Being a professional myself, I was impressed with the way they came across, and I watched Don Harrison the most, in fact not only was this a source of information, it was also entertainment.

I got a call from Lee – Lee was one of the owners of WZAK, a former partner in a broadcasting venture and the godfather of my youngest son – he knew I watched headline news religiously. He told me Don Harrison just died. Have you ever noticed people die several ways, but you never expect it? Even if someone is sick and you expect them to die, you don't expect them to die. Unless you really want that person to die, and you can't wait for a financial gain, or they were a monkey on your back, somehow. Just out of nowhere. It wasn't reported that he was suffering any illness, that I can remember, or that his life was in danger. I expected to still hear Don Harrison to do the news, even now.

He died at the age of 61, same as my father, May 2ⁿᵈ, 1998. He was a member of the original team of news anchors, when CNN Headline News went on the air for the first time. For me, Headline News hasn't been the same. And watch this – to some people, they didn't have a problem with him leaving via dying, and this – some people don't even know he ever existed. Life goes on – with you or without you.

ROGER TROUTMAN / ZAPP

He was the originator, or the creator of the voice-box. To fact it, he made it popular. This was a device that was used, to make a person's vocal ability have an electronic sound that was pleasant. "More Bounce to the Ounce" was the first huge masterpiece, from Zapp featuring Roger Troutman.

I felt an honor in knowing him, he would call me when he recorded a record to let me know he had something new coming out. I was fortunate enough to get his product before anybody else got it. He even respected my opinion of which single to release, if he had several songs that were in the running.

Roger would drive his personal bus/studio to Cleveland, Ohio, from Dayton, Ohio. He would call me, let me know he was downstairs, on Superior Ave, and low and behold there it was, a fabulous vehicle equipped to record a project, on wheels, to go.

With the Zapis family, we had an event called The Anniversary Party, where the admission was free to the public, but they had to get tickets from vendors in the area. It was a win/win project for everyone, especially the listeners. It had to be one of the best events we had, and I think the last public appearance for Zapp.

Roger raved about how our station was the best he had been to, for whatever reason. We were thorough, but his performance, was better than outstanding. And what made it phenomenal was, the audience was wowed and overwhelmed with entertainment.

The word began to spread – Roger was dead. You know how some stories trickle in; it wasn't clear how in the beginning, then somebody he was related to, did it.

Long before us, it was written in the bible that Cain slew Able. Brothers. The closest of the close – you can't get any closer in blood relation than a sibling with the same father and mother. Mother and child are not that close, father and child are not that close – but two children from the same parents have the same blood composition. I don't think that means the same blood type, I'm not in forensics, but it was God's way of showing you that disaster can come from ANYONE, no exceptions. Look up the Akron, Ohio – Milo cosmetics incident, where one brother took the life of the other – do an Internet search, I don't think it is common as all the other tragedies, but there are enough to prove the point of the scripture – anything at any moment from anybody. Restrictions do not apply here.

The news report said that Roger Troutman was murdered by his brother, and then he took his life. Can you imagine the emotional passion of pain that must have existed in Roger's brother's internal structure? Can you imagine the atmosphere when Roger was confronted? You expect to be able to argue to the maximum degree from family and not acquire any physical damage or expect reparation. The normal course of the day. The cost of doing family confrontation. The ability to put the whole swing into it – and miss without embarrassment. The lucky battle to the peak. Like screaming as loud as you can and the release you get, allows you to carry on, like a fuse or pressure valve. Very often needed in the course of many a lifetime.

I was stunned – and because of the kind of person people tell me that I am – I wondered how their mother felt, if she was alive. One son kills another son. I was sad for her, probably more than sad for Roger, although that was a heavy burden on me. Not only did she lose a son because he was murdered, but he was murdered by another son. And on top of that, she loses the second son by his own hands. Three. How do you forget that, ever? Unless your mind blocks that segment of time frames from your memory.

In song – because Roger had touched so many people's lives through his recordings. "I Want to Be Your Man", "Heartbreaker", "Dance Floor", just to kick out several, Roger was the party maker. One of the last things he performed was "California Love" with Dr. Dre and 2Pac. Put one of Roger's records on, and the party was a go.

The excitement created by a Roger Troutman display. Music has a way of piercing the pain you have for something for a moment or so, without any side effectual trails to deal with. You could truly dance your troubles away with a Roger song. Items like this come in your life, and if you are fortunate enough to experience the different levels of association, the sadness of that death has it degrees of intensity –

The songs he sang, the dance we did. The fun that you can see in the master's entertaining us – the happiness – gone. And how about this – never to be duplicated ever again. *I'm sure of it!* Will we laugh again? Of course we will. Will we dance some more? Some of us are dancing now. Will we carry on? Yes, but we have stopped for a moment again – to let someone off the bus of life – and because I knew Roger Troutman...

JON BENET RAMSEY

She stole our hearts, in her little cowboy outfit, didn't she? She hit the media fronts like a tidal wave. To me, it was God's way of showing how sick (and I'm using that term loosely), how sick our society is. For a fact in my eye, she was never missing. She was murdered; we just couldn't find where she was. It had me thinking, probably as most of us were – what if that happened to *my* child? How would *I* feel?

She looked like a little woman, not a little girl. Could that have been the problem? She was well under the age of ten. And how would you have felt as a parent of a missing child, to get blamed for her missing, and later her death.

Was Jon Benet exploited, like so many children are, due to the wants of a parent or older person for monetary or high-attention gains?

The biggest question I asked during that whole period of her missing and later found dead, why just her? Out of all the children that come up missing, or dead, why was she the only one that got that much direction? The death of a child. The missing of a child, or as Nancy Grace says on CNN/Headline news, when a person "goes missing"

Think of all the theft that took place in that period. No graduation for the family through that daughter. If children, no grandchildren or nieces and nephews, if. Watching the child mature and develop as an adult. The crime called, stolen future.

Then recently, a guy who was out of the country, claimed to have been the one who abducted and murdered Jon Benet. Looked like a free plane ride home and attention. Can you imagine claiming to have killed a child and not really doing it – for what purpose could that have been done for?

Go back a few paragraphs. To me, it was God's way of showing how sick (and let me use that word again loosely) how sick the world is. Even though life and living is extremely valuable, as a whole, we place little value on it. How many children have to die before we get a hold of the situation, or is that the plan – not to?

DIANA, PRINCESS OF WALES – LADY DI

It was the SHOCK that was heard around the world. She was the dictionary picture of the definition, peace. She was the dictionary picture of the explanation, love. She appeared to be the gap connector of good to reach out and change the bad. If there was a human dove – it had to be Diana, Princess of Wales. Had to be.

She was with a gentleman in a limousine being chased by the paparazzi. I think that was the first time I ever heard of the paparazzi – which to my understanding, guys (and women, don't want to leave you ladies out), who have cameras, to take pictures of celebs. I always thought they were just photographers.

My first translation was that the paparazzi were some violent organization that set out to kill Diana. When I heard they were just people who took pictures, I thought to myself, why did the limousine flee, as if they were on the run, or knew they were a target for murder? And you know you heard all of the stories and rumors – but let me say this to all of you. What does a sex life, or personal life mean, when the value of the person in question's life means so much to so many people? Why does everything have to have a 'taint' on it? Can't things just be crystal clear?

With that death – *the death of the dove* – it said to me, no one is exempt from tragedy, regardless of your income or social status. There were trillions of tears around the world, because hope was dead for a moment in our vision. The answer suddenly had a question again, and like sheep, all those praying for tranquility were running around lost. The funeral was the biggest I have ever seen. It was probably one of the most publicized death stories in the media – like a reminder something good, has been soiled, let's remind the world of this sadness, so it will sink in deep. Do we still comment on the day of her death – like an anniversary? Why do we do that – what does that do for us, negatively, or can I ask, is there a positive to keep bringing up the dead, over and over?

THE D. C. SNIPER

How can we forget this? And believe me; I am aware that there are a lot of people who never even heard of this. This is not to glorify who did it, but to ask if any of us know any of the names of the people whose lives were taken by these menaces.

And not that I want it to happen, but because we are faced with tragedy in segments, we are not hit by 911, and during the same time, the D.C. Sniper, and during that same time, Katrina, and the Hill Side Strangler - etc, it seems we go through these events, separate from each other, so we don't really get a handle on them, or feel the gripping true bite of them.

During that time, there was a fear that struck out across the country. People from several locations were picked off, unexpectedly, and murdered, for no significant reason except the warped perception of the perpetrator.

I remember talking to a friend of mine, Harry Lyles, who after we discussed the ordeal, spotted the trucks that were given as clues, and we amused ourselves after they found out, that information was incorrect. What a melee that was.

We worry about the terror that may approach us from outside of the country, and rightly so, but can we avoid, the terror within? I can't tell you any name of any of the people that were stolen during that period of time, yet they had to count to somebody, and really; no substitution for their absence. No remedy for their deaths, to me. Had one of those victims been a relative that I was close to, how would I take that, and what are we really doing about anything like this?

Doesn't human life matter? Take all the deaths each year that happen from outside sources, and total the death toll that happens WITHIN THESE COUNTRY WALLS – I'm not talking about any outside countries and their battles, I'm talking about tragedies that happen via murder, or slaughter to Americans from the United States, and the murders that happen within the United States.

I'm sure the totals are higher from within, but you don't see any special group of people rushing to the prevention of that – it is like an open invitation to kill at free will. No matter what. It keeps happening. At free will.

The D.C. Sniper says to me, there are many disgruntled, whatevers. There are hundreds if not thousands of unhappy whomevers. Check the suicide rate. How many people want to spray individuals they don't know, and turn the weapon on themselves? I just heard this the other day – As A Man Thinketh, So Is He. (Women included, please)

How do we correct the disenchanted, the disappointed, the mislead and unhappy? Isn't there something we can do, to cripple the death toll? I see too many unhappy faces. Why can't we accept whatever we have gotten ourselves into, and what's the big deal about being rejected? We need to find a way; we can save people's lives, where they are not victims of theft. We should only die from time – even sickness should be something that happened back in the 90s – don't you think?

RAVENNA, OHIO

You can verify the story, by doing an Internet search. A woman went missing a couple of years back, and the story was troubling to me. She was pregnant. I don't think I will ever see a happy world in my lifetime. And incidents like this conclude it to be true. And briefly, while I have your attention, could you imagine how wonderful a world it would be, if all the people spending time doing negative things, reversed and did positive? But everyone is not seeking a happy home, or peace on earth, some people thrust their lives in chaos. There are persons that bath in disaster with joy. I don't understand it, but I do understand, evil lives.

The husband and father-to-be was looked on as being involved, because there had been a handful of guys who were suspected and convicted of having something to do with the disappearance of their pregnant wives. Do a search on "Laci Peterson".

A woman in Ravenna, Ohio had met a woman and apparently in desperate want of a child of her own, contacted this lady for the vehicle they were selling, knowing the woman was expecting. She killed the woman, took the baby from the woman's body, and buried the woman in her garage. Then when the police department put the data together, and went to the woman's house to arrest her, she shot herself.

I don't really want to go into any theory or really put my opinion out on what I think about the whole situation, but I will say this – How did the people in that neighborhood and the family accept a baby, a new born baby from one day, not pregnant, the next day, BABY? And even though the baby was rescued, that poor woman. And I guess you can tell me, that – that "poor" any1 who has been murdered.

Our thoughts, incorrect that the husband did it. We are wide open to disaster and available prey to the predator. We can't afford to let our guard down, even when we are on peaceful turf, because that's what we've been doing – taking away our forts of protection.

At the time of this incident, I was working in Youngstown, taking the highway, 480, both East and West, which had to pass Ravenna. I even went into Ravenna, to see what kind of town it shaped up to be like, to get gas. It looks like any other town. You see, for the truth of the matter, murder happens EVERYWHERE. It happens in big towns, like New York, Chicago and Detroit, and also happens in small towns, like Orrick, Union Bridge and Ravenna. It happens in the ghettos of the country, as well as the suburbs. On this planet, we can't escape it.

Couldn't adoption been an option? And although the woman who did it is gone, by her own doings, and although it is best to keep moving forward – wouldn't the better picture had been, the baby born to the father and mother that had planned for it?

I don't know if an abundance of death immediately for me would allow me to want to stay here, I think the people that have left me, although I wish they were still around, did so in a timely fashion, although they had nothing to do with it.

If a cousin, or sister was pregnant and this had happened to them, or an aunt, and a child came up missing, and a brother or uncle was shot, and on and on, immediately in my family, it would be tough for me to keep my positive adrenaline flowing profusely. The love of the lives that I have had the pleasure of being affiliated with has kept me floating when I would have drowned had they not existed.

All the questions I had, and I know the questions the others had who followed the story. All the questions that I'm sure that pregnant woman's family still have. I have seen depression. I have seen sad and lonely. I have seen the thirst for love and friendship. I am grateful, that everything I have witnessed has not been a part of my life, and also wish it didn't have to happen to anyone else, but it does, and it will. There will always be a bizarre death story. Tragedies like this, will always be a part of life. And I don't think there is anything we can do about it.

WHEN THE LEVEES BROKE/KATRINA/911

So many things run through my mind, when national tragedies take their toll on the living – and it happens, repetitively. Some of the major janks are man driven – like when a dance floor caved in, and killed a handful of people. It was probably quite a few more than a lot, but more than one is two-many. (Too many). I'm not sure, I think it was a balcony, or the second floor caved into the first floor – too many things happen to keep an accurate account, but I'm sure if you do an Internet search, you can get all the details you are looking for.

What about the bridge that collapsed in California, and all of those travelers were trapped in the ruble. We tipped our hats, and nodded for a silent prayer, then it was on to our daily activities, it ain't me, it ain't anybody related to me, what's the big deal? Care for each other has been stripped, strategically. And you may not like this when I say it (write it), but, THERE IS PROFIT IN DISASTER. Just take a look, just a little closer. Big bucks. Do your research.

When 911 happened, and you can find the book, Rough wRiters, available through Trafford Publishing, it will cover quite a bit about this, in the segment – WHO CAN YOU TRUST?, I want to point out, the way we are coerced into looking at life second or third in the scheme of things. Security can not be blamed for 911, nobody got through using the levels that were set at that time. I think that was explained, ONCE on the Rush Limbaugh show. There wasn't a clear issue of taking the blame off security. It's like you're smoking for years and years – and then wonder why you have cancer. The culprit has already been introduced into your system.

Because of the magnitude of 911 – there were memorials, and pictures of people they couldn't find, and debris, and fumes and smoke and dust and dead. There were people fleeing from their death, jumping from the twin towers, to their death. There were brave firemen, and citizens. There were people that divided on an angry note, terribly distraught; because that was the last time they were going to see the one they really and truly loved and needed to make their lives complete. And through the many people who lost their life during that whole ordeal – there was controversy.

Spike Lee correctly called the situation the name it should be called – WHEN THE LEVEES BROKE. That is what, based on the news stories that I've seen on TV, read on line, in newspapers, that is what did the damage to the most lives when Katrina twisted and turned through the South.

The world watches disaster – I think we crave it. If we didn't, the media would cover onions growing, or kite flying, and they don't. The media is all over disaster like white on snow, or black on the darkest night. We have a never-ending thirst to SEE pain before us. And not to fix it. Not to fix – just to feast, to me.

As the hurricane made it way, crashing to the top for priority in the headlines, we watched. And they were careful not to give us the gory truth all at once, they spoon fed us. When the waters rose above life tolerance, we saw helicopters to the rescue for people and pets. We saw row boats, and efforts being made – Then they started to show floating bodies.

Upon realizing the potential of death that came with this feature, I begin to think about all of the devastation from losing someone. We have barely gotten over 911, or the Oklahoma City Bombing, or the riots for some of us, and media celebrates the anniversary of these events, while the mass marks the recurring date with the pain – the tears. And I'm not saying '*don't cry*' – no, I'm not saying that – I am saying, we don't need to mark the day, to trace the remnant of sorrow, the reflash of anger the agony that comes with this item on the menu – for those who have lost someone, everyday. Everyday you suffer, making attempts to find humor somewhere else. Everyday you struggle to keep going – everyday. Not just when the day comes when it is one year later, or two years later, or three years later – everyday. EVERY – SINGLE – DAY.

When I'm trapped on the freeway, just in traffic – I think of those who lost their life, every time I'm trapped, when they were escaping the city, and ran out of gas, or their vehicles overheated, and the water came and they didn't have anywhere to run.

I think – somebody, some idiot comic is going to use this for material to make people laugh, when you know in your heart – tragedy is no laughing matter. Can you find humor on the journey? Maybe – but too many topics to talk about, to avoid using 911, or Virginia Tech, or Katrina – too many. To use a mass-murderer for comedy. I bet... I bet, if you were to ask any of the family members of the victims, if it is okay to use those negative incidents as routines, they would say no. I can't imagine anyone telling anyone, yeah sure, poke fun at the pain, I still have. But one day – every dark episode will be somebody's bright spot on stage, or on TV.

I watched the rescue attempts. And heard about all the people who stayed. Some of them probably trapped in their attics, as the water rose higher. Did any of you think about that? It could have been you. If you lived where you had to live, based upon your parents' decision or selected by a spouse. You could have been visiting, and caught in the whirlwind.

The folks who had relatives, they couldn't get to them. Teams of those who wanted to help, searching for those who had no one to search for them. Vids who were not at home searching for anything left, family searching for family, and alligators searching for food that had become readily available, because it was human flesh from the negative travesty.

Wading in debris and poison, all the toxins in everything that melted together to create the devastation we all witnessed. And the government that dragged their feet to assist was the story. Remember that nursing home where, if I'm not mistaken, all of the patients died there, because they stayed. Do you remember any of their names?

Emotional residuals that will last forever in some of those minds, based on their connection to the episode. And to think, that this happened almost a hundred years ago. The LEVEES. It was on TV late one night to compare. This means we've learned NOTHING. This means we spent all this time for NOTHING. And although I'm telling you SOMETHING, are YOU going to walk away with NOTHING, too? Maybe someone reading this will think of a way to stop these things, better. To rush to save or assist faster. To get us all on the same page to come together BEFORE, instead of coming together AFTER to talk about it, once again, because it is for sure as you are reading this – it is going to happen again to somebody, somewhere and you know what?

It could be you.

Now.

Are you going to do something about it?

Vickie Lynn Hogan

Today, in fact right now it's 6:02 a.m. Friday morning, April 13, 2007. She has been dead since February 8th of this year, yet the controversial attention has not died down one iota. You're thinking, who is Vickie Lynn Hogan? Her famous and professional name is **Anna Nicole Smith**.

Since she married a financial windfall, through the questionable attack from her deceased husband's relatives until today, she has been an icon of question, in the news. Here is proof that your ethnic origin is not always the reason for your attack or why the spotlight of ill becomes your shadow. And let me say, I'm not lessening the hatred that certain world controllers have for any group that has been singled out – the American Indian, the Jewish community, the African American, our Hispanic population or the Oriental - everything you see is not what you think it is, probably one of the reasons it still exists with a strong current of never, and let me repeat NEVER ever stopping.

She had the fortune of an emotional tango with a multi-millionaire. Probably most of the people that have a problem with her additional benefit of income have the problem; 'they' don't have it. There are probably millions that would have gladly taken her place, and let's include men – there are people out there that would do anything for money. A.N.Y.T.H.I.N.G. Fear Factor and Survivor has proven that.

It would be hard for you to avoid information about Anna Nicole, because she has managed to get news coverage for many things. The marriage, she recently lost her son, which was controversial, she died in February, and there was the dispute on who the father of her young daughter was, which was recently discovered a couple of days ago.

Watching her, said to me, when she was still alive is, it is not always appearance that lands you a job. It is not always the norm of content that gets you ratings. And I'm not putting Anna Nicole down, I know little about what she has to offer, truthfully, but if you are portrayed as something or some kind, it is more than likely, that illustration of your character is what you become.

Anna Nicole Smith comes off to me, in her death, like Marilyn Monroe. The mystique of who her sex life was with. Did she have anything to do with the death of her son? Was she entitled to the money she inherited from the death of her husband? Did she do or overdo drugs? Did she help anyone with the wealth she accumulated? Was she scandalous, or uneducated?

Why did she get the nod with all this hurricane of speculation? Why her? Did she even care what people thought about her?

I don't have an emotional attachment to this death. Except for the news that I watched habitually, I never saw her show, I never concerned myself with her inheritance of wealth, I don't care who the father is. How will any of that benefit me, financially, or mentally? If you need a conversation topic, wa-la! But other than that, some people are going to get a fortunate enhancement nod, that's the way life is. People are going to die everyday – some you'll know, most you won't. But everyone that dies, will not have an effect on you – and that's okay. Death does not sadden everyone. There is no specific way you are supposed to act, or supposed to do. The way you are made up, what your character is, determines how you react or the way you respond, when time expires on someone. Some cry for someone they never met, and others feel nothing for cherished loved ones, there are varieties of the way people display what they are going through.

Anna Nicole Smith (Vickie Lynn Hogan) was 39 years of age, when she died.

Virginia Tech

April 18, 2007 – CNN Headline News, reporting the aftermath of the incident that took place, April 16ᵗʰ, from a lone gunman at the school campus, from my research, two different locations on campus, then self destruction. I'm not going to mention the guy's name, just the fact that he was Asian. Thirty Three (33) people were killed, the gunman inclusive.

I see the sadness that comes when something like this happens. And there are so many things going on and on in my head. As I use to say years ago, when the perp takes their own life, as that has happened – why don't they just take their own life, and spare the others? 32 – Thirty Two would have been spared this time, along with those injured.

And we focus on WHERE THE GUN WAS PURCHASED, why focus on that? It could have been ANY GUN, but it was someone's daughter, someone's son. It was somebody's specific sister, a brother who had a name; and a relationship with people. What difference does it make, where the gun came from? What if he had used his bare hands? See how idiotic we focus on things? Why can't we REALLY, and I mean REALLY work on preventing this? Why do we dissect these projects incorrectly?

Mark my words – MARTIAL LAW is coming hard on us. We may not feel its nasty bite within the next few moments, but you MARK MY WORDS it is coming. It may take years, BUT; as tragedy propels forward, and THE LACK OF IMMEDIATE LAW dominates the forefront, the mass is going to demand it, in a manner of speaking.

Why do we hero-ize the villain, and gutter the victims? All of those people, who were related to the slain, will have a permanent memory of what could have been – marriages of those people in that ceremony. Grandchildren. There could have been a government official that could have turned some positive things. A doctor who probably would have discovered a cure of a fatal. An inventor of a product. We have all been robbed.

As the tears flowed heavily down the faces of those closest, here we go again. Columbine was the granddaddy of them all, years back, now we have this massacre. Each of those 32, thirty-two people had a future. And I'm willing to bet, they have all died in vain. We are no closer to a cure or remedy. It's just news. BULLETIN! BREAKING NEWS! The media CRAVES this frenzy. They LOVE disaster – can't wait to dash out and get that scoop!

And I can't place the blame solely on the media, they are only feeding you want you desperately desire – *hell: through a looking glass*. We want to get as close to it as possible, without getting any blood on our hands. Maybe these heinous acts of violence make us feel better about our own miserable lives. Maybe seeing someone take a bullet, watching people in sheer sorrow, is joy in our twisted minds, just maybe....

Until it happens to us.

Now what?

A news reporter, or weather man committed suicide; just a couple of weeks before this, in Florida. We are not interested in mental stability. Let's say ALL of these happenings are CASUALTIES OF MEDIA WAR. What would we report if things like this didn't happen, how to grow turnips? Move over Martha Stewart, there is not enough bloodshed on your illustrations – Christopher Lowell hasn't got a chance!

I don't have all of the statistics, but how many parents lost their only child? How many of the lot were the first in the family to go to college? How many mini-milestones were being accomplished by the crew of 32?

Think of the handsome young men, and the beautiful young women who were snuffed out, I do not know what I would do if I had a child attending Virginia Tech and they were one of the victims. How many lost smiles and warm hugs have been stolen from the thief of future dreams come true?

Now you won't be able to see the child of your child that reminds you of your child who has grown when they were a child. We need government rule. You see, if you have had the terror-guard in place, if you have a militarical force, did you see The Minority Report, featuring Tom Cruise. We are being set up for the taking – the spike of the volleyball is at our feet, stinging and burning our tomorrow to a crisp, with the corners singed.

The shooter raged against women and rich kids. Just think if everyone who had a problem with women and rich kids did this. Just think if all of us acted on the things that ticked us off.

Ever notice that very little attention is given to the victims? Most of the spotlight is on THE SHOOTER, the KILLER. Why is our world like this? Ask yourself, how many victims do you remember by name, and how many killers do you know? I am not mentioning any murderer, but you think about it – sure there are famous targets, like John Lennon, or Abraham Lincoln, but their killers got more of the attention. John F. Kennedy's assassin, and Martin Luther King Jr.'s assassin. And that name – ASSASSIN. Doesn't it have a nice ring to it? Like it's positive?

Ross Alammedine, 20. Jamie Bishop, 35. Brian Bluhm, 25. Ryan Clark, 22. Austin Cloyd (F), 19. Jocelyne Couture-Kowak (F). Daniel Perez Cueva, 21. Kevin Granata, 46. Matthew Gwaltney, 24. Caitlin Hammaron (F), 19. Jeremy Herbstritt, 27. Rachel Hill (F), 18. Emily Jane Hilscher (F) 19. Jarrett Lee Lane, 22. Matthew La Porte, 20. Henry Lee. Liviu Lebrescu, 76. G.V. Loganathan, 51. Partahi Lombantoruan, 34. Lauren McCain (F), 20. Daniel O'Neil, 22. Juan Ramon Ortiz, 26. Minal Panchal (F), 26. Erin Peterson (F), 18. Michael Pohle, 23. Julia Pryde (F) 23. Mary Karen Read (F), 19. Reema Samaha (F), 18. Waleen Shaalan, 32. Leslie Sherman (F), 20. Maxine Turner (F), 22. Nicole Regina White (F), 20.

My bet to you is, if you don't know any of the before mentioned personally, you will forget them. But you won't forget the guy who did it. One year from the day it happened, Monday, April 16th, 2007, there will be an anniversary. They may contact a couple of the relatives of the deceased, but the focus will be on that guy who pulled the trigger. And now we find out, the guy was supposed to have had mental treatment. He sent correspondence to the police. MARTIAL LAW, I'm telling you, we are headed for DOME CITY PROTECTIVE LIVING, where everything is under control – EVERYTHING. Catch DEMOLITION MAN with Wesley Snipes and Sylvester Stallone. Everything under a glass. Robocop III (or 2) – We are headed for an iron fist of discipline.

Think of all the funerals – All the tears, not just now, but for every person that had a connection with one of the '32' – Some of them were best friends to somebody – we don't really think about all that we have had stolen – and months from now, it will be like this never really happened.

Watch comedians spawn their jokes and monologues in reference to this, and here's the punch-line, they will get a laugh. And granted, I know it is great to move on, and laugh again, but we don't have to laugh at this... do we?

This DYING THING

HOPE

hearing other people's experiences

I will share with you several of my experiences with death. I will preface this by telling you I was raised a Catholic, but not strict. I no longer have any religious ties. I have not raised my children with any religion or church; but have not discouraged them from making their own choices.

My first experience involved my paternal grandmother. She was old, and lived with us for a good part of my childhood, but lived the last year with my Aunt. I was probably 10 or so when she passed. Honestly, it really did not affect me because we were not close- she wasn't the nicest woman. But one night after she passed, I had a "dream" that was so vivid and felt so real, it was incredible. I saw her and was stunned, because I knew she was dead. I didn't have any fear; and all the normal questions a 10 year old would have were buzzing in my head, like "I thought you were dead!" "What are you doing here?" etc. But the words that came out of my mouth were "Are you happy?" This was a question I did not think, just spoke. And she said, "Yes, tell everyone I am happy."

I had an uncle who "died" during open heart surgery, but ended up surviving the surgery. He said it was the most incredible experience, and had no fear of dying and welcomed it when the time was right.

When Harry's mom passed, our son Bubby was almost 3 years old. And right after she passed, and for a couple of weeks after, he would "see" her. He would point her out to us, tell us to say hi to her and talk to her. Of our 3 kids, it was Bubby she loved most. When Harry's dad passed he was in Indiana- Harry and I were home in Georgia sitting in our kitchen talking. We had gotten news earlier in the day that he was doing better. As we were talking at the table, our back door burst open with a strong, cold wind and blew right through us both. I felt his dad's spirit in that cold air, but didn't tell Harry what I felt because I didn't want to seem morbid. After all, we were just told he was doing better. About 20 minutes later, we got the call that he had passed about 20 minutes earlier.

A couple of weeks ago, I had dinner with a friend who lost her 20 year old brother about 2 years ago. She said when he "visits" she feels cold air... And she definitely feels his presence on occasion and gets "gifts" from him.

I don't believe in "religion" - I feel it's more important to live your life in a positive, loving way.

G

even after someone has left this earth, you can still love them until the day you die...

Monday, January 29, 1968. It's a day that I'll always remember. I was only 13 years old. Not just any 13 year old mind you but a wide eyed know it all 13 year old with a pretty good acne problem. It was a beautiful and unseasonably warm day in my home town of Winston-Salem, North Carolina. Monday's at my home where always pinto bean day. That's a day that my Mom made the most delicious meal of the week. She cooked a big pot of pinto beans with a fresh ham hock inside along with fresh corn bread and stewed cabbage. If you're not from the south, pinto beans is a staple and every Monday was a day to look forward to just because of the food!

The temperature outside was in the 70s and for a January day even in the south, that was a really nice day. It still looked like January as I recall because it was a bit overcast. My Mother Elizabeth and my sister Anne had decided to take advantage of the nice weather that day and go out for a bike ride around 4pm. I was home just kind of goofing off as I liked to do pretty much every day after school. Suddenly without warning there was a thunderous knock on the door of my home on Talcott Avenue and a repetitive ringing of the doorbell as if someone was in panic. I opened the door and a neighbor kid was out of breath panting saying there had been an accident and my Mother was hurt. I ran out the door and followed the kid running seemingly in slow motion.

About a block away, my Mom was lying in the street quivering like an animal. I could see brain matter oozing out of her head. There was a lot of blood. Neighbors had gathered round her. Someone had put a blanket over her but everyone was saying not to move her and an ambulance was en route. My sister Anne was crying and everyone around her was extremely upset. My Mom was someone that everyone loved in the neighborhood and so there was a realization that she was in a lot of trouble. My sister had described her falling off the bike hitting the side of her head on the street curb.

We waited what seemed like an eternity for the ambulance to arrive. In fact it took the ambulance over 45 minutes to arrive. We lived in a rural area and we later learned that the drivers had got lost on their way to pick up my Mother. When they arrived, they secured her onto a stretcher and put her on board. My sister and I went in the ambulance with my Mom to the hospital. On the way, the paramedics were working on my Mom trying to stabilize her. She was still quivering but unconscious.

When we arrived at the hospital, my Dad was there waiting. He had been contacted at work to go and meet us at the hospital. My Dad ran a gas station called the Downtown Garage. He was in his navy blue filling station uniform. He was crying and wondering what took so long. We all wondered that. They put us all in a room to wait.

Do animals deal with death,
the same way we do?
Do they mourn?
Are they sad?
Are they stopped for minutes,
or weeks, sometimes months
and forever -
or do they immediately pick up and go forward?

We were there for quite some time waiting to see what was going to happen with my Mom. A doctor slowly opened the door and came inside the room. He looked at my Dad and said, "I'm sorry, we did everything we could, she's gone". It was just like someone hit me over the head with a hammer. I was stunned and in shock. For the first time in my life I heard my Dad weep in a way that I'll never forget. It was long, deep and groanful. I've never heard anything like it before.

My Mother, Elizabeth Sapp Newton was only 49 years old. She was a wonderful loving Mother and wife who had everything to live for. Of course we all ask "why" but we'll never really know that on this side of eternity. I do know that because my Mother trusted in Jesus that she is in a better place. That does give me comfort. My Dad has since gone on to be with the Lord and I picture the two of them dancing in paradise and that gives me more comfort. I also think that they look down here and they must be very proud of what they helped produce in their lifetime here. The bible says that life is like a vapor. It's here today and it's gone tomorrow. I believe that we where created to be instruments of God's grace, peace, and love. When we're not living for here and now but are storing up treasures in eternity then we are really living.

That's how God created us because we are eternal creatures. Bob Dylan said it so well. "Gotta Serve Somebody". We're either serving the Lord and doing His will or we're serving the God of this world and when we do that we lose. God wants his creatures to be the head and not the tail.

He wants us to be lenders to many nations, to feed and cloth the poor, and to love our neighbor as our self. He is our shepherd and we shall not want of anything. He also wants us to love him and put him first in all that we do. When we seek Him first and His righteousness then the abundant life that Jesus promised will be ours.

All I've ever wanted out of this life is love, peace, and joy. Real love, real peace and real joy are not of this world. They are manifest in His holy spirit that dwells inside of me. Death doesn't concern me that much anymore because I do have this wonderful blessed assurance that nothing can ever separate me from the love of the Lord. I also know that God has removed the sting of death through his son Christ Jesus. As for me losing my Mom at such a young age. The bible says that ALL things work together for good to those who love God and are called according to His purpose. I came into a personal relationship with Jesus when I was 18.

Would I be the person I am today if it where not for being a Christian? Absolutely not. Would I be the person I am today if it weren't for the life of my Mom? Absolutely not. Would I be the person I am today if it weren't for the death of my Mom? Absolutely not. ALL things are working together for good because I do love the Lord and I know that I'm called according to his purpose.

Tom K. Newton

These two pictures are the same. It is a picture I took in Tampa, on the Hillsborough river. You can see a better picture in the smaller of the two. The larger picture, is out of focus. Often, when we make a big deal out of something, it becomes distorted. On many things and issues, we should learn to really get the value, out of the smaller things - the simple things. Take advantage of your life, while you are still living it.

Lynn Tolliver, jr.

FOR ME DEALING WITH DEATH YOU HAVE TO BE SELFLESS AND WHEN YOU LOVE SOMEONE IT'S VERY DIFFICULT. IT TOOK ME A COUPLE OF YEARS TO BE ABLE TO DEAL WITH MY MOTHER/BEST FRIEND, SHE WAS LIKE NO OTHER AND CAN AND WILL NEVER BE REPLACED. SHE DIED SUDDENLY ON HER WAY HOME FROM WORK. I DIDN'T GET A CHANCE TO SAY GOODBYE AND I REALLY HATE THAT.

THANK GOD FOR MY WONDERFUL GRANDMOTHER BECAUSE WITHOUT HER I COULD NOT HAVE MADE IT WITHOUT MY MOTHER. I STILL GRIEVE DAILY FOR MY MOTHER AND NOW BOTH OF THEM ARE GONE AND I FEEL SO LOST BUT THEY ARE NOT SUFFERING NOT SHEDDING A TEAR NOT IN ANY PAIN AND THEY ARE WITH EACH OTHER.

TWO OF THE GREATEST WOMEN ARE GONE AND WILL DEFINITELY BE MISSED UNTIL I'M ABLE TO JOIN THEM

VERDELLE, YOUR NIECE

mind inspirations

I lost my mother may 29th 2005. She was almost 75 years old. She had a cancer growth in her throat that cut her airway off. But I had a chance to spend time with her before it was over. I wanted to believe that she was going to be ok, even her doctor told that it would happen any day. At that point she lasted two weeks after that. The last time I saw her I thanked her for having me and all the things she did for me and how much I loved her and I would be back in St. Louis in July, and she said I will not be here. That was weird for me because I did not want to believe it. Then she told me "peace be with you" and I love you my son so, I came back to Jacksonville to work.

I called her every day all week and she sounded like she was getting better she said it too, that made me feel better but that Sunday I did not talk to her and as I was going to do a club I got the call from home that she was gone. I went and did the club because I know she would have said go make that money boy! Mama believed in hard work! I can say at this point in my life I miss my mother almost every day and it hurts deep but, I know she is not in more pain or discomfort anymore and I will see her again.

JoJo-
Afternoons
WSOL/V-101.5 Jacksonville

My mother had not been feeling good for a very long time. She had a diseased heart. Over weight, she loved to light one up. She refused to take her doctor's orders to watch what she ate and exercise. Wasn't about to let a doctor tell her what to do. She said smokin' cigarettes and eatin' made her happy, plus it kept her from losing her mind! I think my mother would have rather gone to a witch doctor, than to fool around with one in a hospital. I knew the day was coming when I would lose her, I just didn't know when. It was painful. Everyday, I thought about how bad my mother was feeling and yet, she was still helping my disabled sister raise her two young children.

My mother knew her time was coming. She talked about dying during our usually long conversations of how to solve the problems of the world. One night she said, she was ready "to go" because she was feeling so bad. I couldn't believe that my mother didn't want to live anymore! I couldn't ee-ven stand to hear her talk about it. Knowing she was not afraid and was ready to die, liked to killed me!

Yep... She pretty much made her peace with God. I knew she was ready to go. It troubled me most of the time. I felt she had so much to live for, even at the age of 73. I knew my time with her was running out. I wanted my mother to know how much she meant to me, and savored our moments together. We would fuss, argue, and have a good time! I told her how much I loved her, and that she was my best friend.

I even told her of how much I'd miss her once she was gawn. I did what ever I could to help her but felt what ever I did, it just wasn't enough. No one ever knew how distraught I really was about my mother preparing herself to meet her maker.

I tried to prepare myself emotionally for the day the angels would come. Mommy died on February 1, 2005 of a heart attack. I tried to be brave and hold my head up. I told myself that I was okay with her dying and this is what is supposed to happen in life. Besides, she was finally at peace, no longer worried with the troubles of life, or the troubles of this world. With all the thoughts I had before her death, nothing prepared me for the devastation I felt when she died or the loneliness that I feel to this day.

Amazing. My relationship with my mother changed over the course of time. I came to know her as more than just my "Mommy". I came to know her as a person. I came to know and understand her as a woman. My mother was fair in complexion. Daddy often called her "Red". We called her "Chief" too, because she ruled us with an iron fist. My mother did not play! She sacrificed herself over, and over again, always putting her family first as mothers and women often do. Sometimes, I think she did that to her detriment. I wish there was more that I could have done for her. I wish there was more that she could have done for herself.

If only she could be here to see how my youngest nephews, have grown. They will be 16 this year. She had other grandkids and great grandkids too, but she loved and cared for my sister's children like they were her own. I hope they will hold on to the memories of their grandmother. I hope the things that she instilled in them will carry them into their adult lives. Things like good character, integrity, the importance of love and family, and appreciating the simple things in life.

My mother! She was the best friend I'd ever had. She was my confidante. She gave me courage to be the "strange bird" that I am. Other than God, I never trusted anyone as I trusted my mother. I loved her logic. One time Mommy said, "People talk about how life is not fair. Life is fair! It's just so un-cool."

My mother was a very intelligent woman, and she was always humor ready. She was "a bad motor scooter", as she would say. We had a lot of fun with her. We had some very difficult times together too. I learned a lot from my mother. I learned, and understood more about her, even after she died. I miss her more with the passing of each day. My mother's death left a big ole hole in my heart. One that I am still trying to fill.

I wonder... What was my mother thinking right before she died? Where did she go after she died? What happened to her soul? Where did she go? I look around. I see her in the trees, a sunlit sky. I see her in me.

Lady Skill
Cleveland, Ohio
March 28, 2007

In memory of ....

I have had to bury so many of my family members starting with my Dad when I was 9 years old. I remember my grandfather dying when I was even younger but I did not understand the finality of death. My father was only 31 years old when he succumbed to a fatal heart attack. We were waiting for him to come home from the hospital, making ready a huge dinner with family and friends bustling about our project apartment on that chilly Valentine's Day. My younger sisters were playing a ball rolling game having the strangest conversation about how daddy was not coming home he was going to be asleep in his Sunday suit and how momma was going to be mad at him. I half way paid attention but thought they are just little kids playing.

The next day one of our parents' friends came over wringing her hands and crying uncontrollably saying to our mother how sorry she was, could she do anything for her.

As the older children (my older sister my brother and I) came barreling down the stairs, we see my mother bolt for the phone with her sister standing next to her and our uncle next to them both when our mother just collapsed to the floor. I had never heard such weeping and screaming in my life I had never seen my mother cry... I did not know she could cry, my mother was invincible! She could do anything! And there she was crying and screaming for our father...He was DEAD. She was mad he was in his Sunday suit. I remember I was hysterical at his funeral, I had to be carried out in my white dress as my pressed hair was wring wet from my screaming and crying when I saw him in that casket.

I loved my daddy so much and to lose him so early in my life, I did not think I would ever recover, the loss of my father and the cloak of seeing my mother in so much pain.

It was a defining time in my young life as I decided then that I would take life and live not be sad when someone dies to love them now, not wait til later because you or they may not have a later. I learned that even your parents are flawed as we all fall short of the Glory of GOD. I learned very early that there is a living force controlling the universe and it was not me.

Though our dad was a self proclaimed atheist he made sure we grew up with a Christian upbringing...he would say, "Just in case there is a GOD, I want my children protected"

Peace...
Mother Love
Author
HALF THE MOTHER TWICE THE LOVE,
My Journey to Better Health with Diabetes
(Atria Books 2006)
ADA Volunteer
CO Chair of ADA African American Task Force, LA
dLife TV/Correspondent
www.motherlove.us
www.YTB.com/motherlovetravelbiz

Cherish the moments in life you spend together, with people who are close to you. Do we use the term, "friend" incorrectly? Do we miss out on friendships and family ties, because we're blinded by perils thrown before us? Do we allow life to just pass us by, and realize too late, we could have had a go at it? Let's take time, out - and discover advantages life has to offer, when you're on the right track.

Lynn Tolliver, jr.

I had a friend who committed suicide. We were not close although we shared many good times and even quiet moments.

I had no idea that my friend was suffering from depression. I had no idea that she was taking medication. I had no idea she had an eating disorder. I did know that she had graduated at the top of her law school class and was an excellent attorney. I did know that she was an emphatic jogger. I did know that she was considered attractive by everyone. I did know that she was alone. I did know that she considered me a good friend, maybe not close but a good friend. I say all of this to say that I miss her even eight years later as I write this, I miss her. I only have one regret and that is that I didn't ask...are you in pain? As I write this now, as corny as it may sound I have learned to watch for signs in people I consider a friend...I ask, are you in pain? I may not have the remedy, my Psychology degree does not guarantee that I have the answer but as a Christian and as a man, I have learned the hard way that is is okay to ask, are you in pain and to let them know, I am here for you day and night. It is an overused cliché but one that I believe in now.

Strength, Honor and Blessings,
James Hinton
www.myspace.com/talos65

Death is so overwhelming; it can really take its toll on you and at times leave a lot of unanswered questions. On February 18, 2007 my friend passed away. I knew that she was sick; she had cancer and had been in the hospital three weeks before she died. Although I knew that she was sick, I was devastated to hear that she had died, see because she and I had a disagreement about something and had decided that we would not speak to each other again. The last things I said to her was that she was wicked, bitter and at times hateful and that she had way too much going on in her life to always have some mess going on.

Then it was rumored that she had brain cancer, if this is true, it would explain her strange behavior and paranoia over the years then everything started to seem so frivolous. But now I will never get a chance to make up with her because she is gone forever, yeah I know that I can always talk to her in spirit, but for me, it is just not the same. I am learning a hard lesson from this, and that lesson is that we, I have to learn how to LET STUFF GO! Get over it and move on, because it is not worth it. My friend is gone and all because of a stupid disagreement, I never got a chance to tell her how much she meant to me, and now I never will.

Thank you, for allowing me to share this with you.

Bridgett T. Sanders

Young Girl

She runs and laughs as children do, such a silly girl.

Playing children's games with such joy, so innocent is

she.

But innocence cannot remain for this girl,

She must grow and face her destiny.

And so she blossoms to woman, yet still a foolish girl.

Young girl of yesterday has lost her way.

Her future burning bright before her,

The child's light could not stay.

Love of life now becomes love of Mary Jane,

And sweet Mary leads her to a foolish boy.

From this threesome comes a baby free of bane,

For a time all are blessed with joy.

By Mary's dark desire, bliss soon departs.

By vehicles unknown and raging fire, poor girl has gone

away.

She left behind many broken hearts,

Young girl just could not stay.

Marcus Richardson-Lighty
3/15/07
Final Poem

time is precious....
don't waste it -

Sometimes it is just like yesterday or an hour ago...the numbness still lingers in my body the emptiness in my stomach and oh how it aches..It started August 1, 1998 a mild Saturday morning the phone rang and it's my husband's niece she is crying and she is very sad she ask to speak with my husband Marvin. I can still visualize him setting in the kitchen chair he takes the telephone and I see his face change and he says thanks for letting us know and he hangs the phone up and looks at me and says that was Dina she says my Aunt Dorothy died and we should all meet at her house.

My oldest daughter Keytsa was on a trip in NY. My youngest daughter Kimberly was all dressed to go to the amusement park and she was waiting for her date, I made a call to Marvin's sister and told her we would pick her up and we would all go to his Aunt Dorothy's house..Now this was the beginning of, "wow I had night mares over and over again." Marvin decides that he has to wash his Van before we pick up his sister, fine with me I say..to the car wash we go...while we are in the car- wash he complains that his teeth feel funny and his jaw is dropping and every thing in his face feels strange...this is while we are in the car wash (in side while the car is washing) I thought that it was just another head ache or something "actually he was having a heart attack and I did not know it.

After we pulled out of the car wash I asked if he wanted me to drive back home he said no and he pulled into the driveway of the store and told me to go in and get him some aspirins and water and I did..He took them and let the seat of the van back and took a rest and then he drove home.

As soon as we got home he went upstairs to lie across the bed..minutes later my daughter hollered out mommy daddy is having a heart attack...just as she said this her friend pulled up in his truck...I ran to the door and told him I needed him to take Marvin to the hospital.

Marvin walked down the stairs holding his heart...into the truck and down to Bedford Hospital we went...into the wheelchair and into the hospital I waited outside the door...finally the doctors told me it was not good and he was going to have to be life flighted to Hillcrest Hospital...."you know what??? I was told later that my husband's heart stop beating twice while he was in the air – ok.... I made a long distant call to Tuskegee where my mother lived and told her what was going on and that Marvin had a heart attack and would she please come and help me take care of him and she said yes..She would fly here and do that..I called her back and said she did not need to come right away but the following month would be great..(Now I had no idea that my mom was possibly sick too. If she was, she would not have told me at that time anyway, because she would not want to worry me. She knew that my husband had been on dialysis for 6 years and me being her only child she did not want me to make a choice between the two of them.

My mom came to Cleveland and stayed with us. She stayed with Marvin everyday and went to dialysis with him. He was on the machine 3 hours a day, Monday Wednesday Friday....Marvin mentioned to me that my mom seemed to be having bad headaches and that something must be wrong.

I took her to the hospital one morning in December, only to find out she had a mild stroke..later diagnosed as A CANCEROUS TUMOR in her sinus. She was put on radiation everyday except the wk end. My mom lived Jan99 to May 23 99 and she died....May 25 1999 I am sitting in my kitchen writing her obituary when once again my daughter says mommy DADDY is having a heart attack.

We called 911 they took my husband out on the stretcher he had tears in his eyes and he kept saying Verdell I am so sorry...He felt so bad he knew my mother had just died 2days before as they carried him out and life flighted him once again to Hillcrest hospital tears running down my eyes and my two daughter eyes we rushed to the hospital...Once again the doctors told me they lost him and brought him back...4 months later my husband of 30 years died in my bed of all the times he left and came back this was it.

I held his hand and kept eye contact until it was over. My house shook and then there was silence...The Lord put me in a state of mind I cannot explain, I was so numb it seemed just so unreal that my momma would die and 4 months later my darling husband, my children's father, a good man who worked to give us good things would be gone even though he had been sick for 7yrs on dialysis he was gone.

I typed all of this to say I love the Lord...only the Lord knew how much I could take ..I believe that he allowed Marvin to have the heart attack Aug 1, 1998 to bring my mother to Cleveland so that I could take care of her and she would be here in Cleveland when she died and it would have been too much for me if Marvin had died two days after she did (too much for me).

I believe God was in the plan..he allowed me to grieve a couple of months and then it was Marvin's time - I hurt so bad and I still do, But I am a true believer in the Lord Jesus Christ and that is how I am living today...God Bless You ..

Your Kuzzin' Verdell Captain Warren

The first time Death knocked on my mind's door, was the Ides of March 1995.

Death arrived to serve papers on my Grandmother but; Death had called ahead, five months prior.

Death graced me with "extra" time with Granny like Death understood the pain I would feel by taking her straightaway,

Death allowed Granny to teach me her "final lessons." She showed me how deeply she loved me as.....every breath she took was for.....me....and.....her breath was heavy...like the earth's gravitational pull. All my life she....loved me this way.

Death gave her time to teach me to be strong in life and death.

Death gave her time to teach me to be courageous in life and death.

Death gave her time to show me how to live and die.

Death gave me a priceless gift in
allowing my grandmother to die in my arms while she
fought to tell me that she loved me, one last time.

This was my greatest gift of ALL, a wrapped blessing of
privilege and pride.

Death ultimately, will serve my papers.

I am comforted to know that **Alpha Rita DuVall** will do
for me as I did for her and accompany me to the
doorstep of the universe.

This is my Dying Thing.

Synthia Hathorn

He Can Hear Me

By Venus Jones

www.venusjones.com

My alarm and my heart kept the same time
But my tardiness was not the biggest crime
I woke up to the dreaded call

"He was in the hall."
"Where, at school?"
"He got shot down!"
"Where?"
"Didn't you see the front page or hear? His home."
"Oh my dear."
But he doesn't mess around, barely 5 feet tall
He lay surrounded by yellow tape in a pool of blood
upstairs in the hall
In their brand new home in the hall
His crime was protecting his mother from a fatal love
affair
I dropped the phone and fell to the floor
There was no one there to care

That cuckoo male "friend" happened to pull the trigger
on himself, too
At fourteen I was in total disbelief that this could
happen to anyone I knew
The bark of my youth fell off on a manic Monday
God took his child Ricky at a sweet and sour 16 away
I walked in slow motion through the misery and moans
of children at his wake
His mother was the dove of peace in front of a dark

blue lake

What I took from his coffin is what I want you to take from me

If I die tomorrow I want you to be everything I didn't have time to be

Take a moment

To reach in the grave and grab every unfulfilled dream you see

Like moss his gifts of words grew on me

He could make you laugh if no one else could

On him I would confide because he understood

One of the friendliest boys in the neighborhood

He was the essence of cool

I use his early departure as a tool

Never would he dismiss a pretty sight so I observe day and night

His life purpose was fulfilled when he fell like a branch from our tree

He risked life and limb because for him love meant family

Actress/Model/Poet/Voice
(Author of SHE ROSE)
http://www.venusjones.com –

Life can be tough. If you live a normal life with a course of simplicity, you can experience as much sorrow as the adventurer that travels on the wild side. If you don't want to spend a long life in sorrow and depression, change the way you think. Often people who are close to us, die when we are not ready for them to. I can't tell you how to prevent the pain, but if you live life, the best & positive of your ability, I don't think you'll suffer as much, if you don't.

Lynn Tolliver, jr.

I FACED DEATH THROUGH A PERSONAL EXPERIENCE OF MY OWN WHEN A STALKER EMPTIED THEIR GUN ON ME AND MY CAR WHEN I ARRIVED AT WORK AT THE RADIO STATION I WORKED FOR RIGHT BEFORE MY SHIFT. THOUGHOUT MY LIFE MANY FAMILY MEMBERS AND FRIENDS HAVE PASSED ON USUALLY THREE TO FIVE WITHIN A FEW WEEKS APART.

I LEARNED THROUGH MY NEAR DEATH EXPERIENCE AND THE DEATH OF OTHERS THAT I HAD TO GO THROUGH A PROCESS THAT INCLUDES GRIEVING, MOURNING AND HEALING. YOU CAN NOT GET TO THE HEALING UNTIL YOU HAVE ALLOWED YOURSELF TO GO THROUGH THE FIRST TWO. HEALING CANNOT BE MEASURED IN TIME BECAUSE FOR EACH ONE OF US THE LENGTH OF TIME WILL BE DIFFERENT, BUT I DO KNOW JUST AS THERE IS A BEGINNING THERE IS ALSO AN ENDING AND GOD MARKS THE TIME AND THE HOUR.

GOD WILL HEAL YOU IF YOU ALLOW HIM TO. LET HIM INTO YOUR LIFE AND BELIEVE IN THE PROMISE HE MADE TO US IN HEBREWS 13:5, "I WILL NEVER LEAVE YOU NOR FORSAKE YOU."

PEOPLE COME AND GO BUT GOD AND THE GOD WITHIN US THAT GIVES US STRENGH REMAINS. HOLD ON TO HIS MIGHTY WORD AND LIVE EACH DAY TO BE A BLESSING TO SOMEONE ELSE WHO NEEDS YOUR LOVE NOW.

MIMI BROWN
THE COMFORT ZONE

I would like to send my condolences for the loss of your mother and for all the ones you loved who are no longer with you in body.

This dying thing means many emotions and feelings. It is mind blowing. To experience the death of someone near and dear to you will take you through so many different emotions and mood swings. Death can bring on sorrow, joy, relief, sadness and anger.

Like right now. I am sitting at work tonight listening to Gerald Levert's new CD. His family crossed my mind and I wonder how they are doing. We recently suffered a great loss in my family. My beloved cousin only 48 years of age passed away in his sleep. I shed a few tears for all of us left behind.

With each death that I live through the affect it has on me and my reaction is different. At this point I have lost both parents, grandparents, great-grand mother, great uncles and aunts, cousins, some friends I met during my childhood and some I met as an adult. Thank god all my siblings are still here.

My cousin passed away on Tuesday March 27th 2007. My first reaction was disbelief. It is the kind of news you don't want to hear so there is a need to make sure that what you heard was correct. I had to ask the questions "What?" and "Are you sure?" after the immediate denial reality set in but I didn't cry. He died after saying he was tired and going to take a nap. His brother found him in his bed.

We were in the same class in kindergarten. He was the same age as me and his birthday is April 7th. A fun loving,

Pamela Delphyne Dees

loud, 6 feet 5 inches tall man who was loved by many and would give the shirt off his back. Five years ago he got out of prison after 15 years. Two more months he would have been off parole and finally free to travel anywhere. He had already made arrangements to come to our 30th annual family reunion in Detroit this summer. He missed 15 reunions, holidays and birthdays and births in the family because of his incarceration. My god he and his siblings just lost their mother in January! So unfair!

This makes me so angry. Not at god (I trust and have faith in god to get me through these life challenges.) Can't be mad at god. The anger is directed to me. I took for granted that he would be here when I had the time to call more or visit him. Anger is the affect this death has on me at this stage in my life. He was supposed to grow old. We were supposed to tell our stories for 25th time to all the youngsters or to anyone who would listen. I finally cried when I saw his body at the funeral home, then at his funeral and cried on the freeway heading back to Georgia. I loved my cousin dearly and will miss him. Never take another persons life for granted.

Mommy: A loss from long ago.

As mentioned before both my parents are deceased. The grieving process is different in the fact that I lost one parent as a child and the other as an adult. The span of time between their deaths doesn't matter. I miss them very much. Death is such a major traumatic event for a child. I

Pamela Delphyne Dees

think adults tend to believe when a child losses his parent they don't grieve. We move on accept the new man or woman to replace the one that died and everything is alright. We go outside and play and you hear us laughing and carrying on but there is confusion and hurt and shock over what has happened. Children expected to forget their deceased parent and not speak of them ever again. I was told that my mother is dead and I have to forget her because I have a new mother now. Call her mommy now.

For a while I forgot I once had a mother. I was 27 and a mother of a three year old when one of my co-workers asked why I never talk about my mother. All my parent stories were about my father. I actually answered her with "Oh, my mother died when I was a child." It suddenly occurred to me that I had a mother at one time. How could I forget that very important part of life?

On Tuesday March 17, 1970, I suffered a loss in my life that no child should have to deal with but the sad reality is some will. My mother died in the 28th year of her life. Mommy left behind me and my three younger sisters ages 10, 8 and 5 years old. I was eleven. Before I go into the affect her death had on me I have to touch on the illness she suffered and died from. It had a huge impact on me as well.

Mommy was sick with what I would come to know as breast cancer. There were times she would be coughing like she had a cold, or would get so hot that she would roll down the car windows in the dead of winter. Her behavior was weird to me and sometimes I felt she didn't think about

Pamela Delphyne Dees

83

us when the windows were rolled down and we would be freezing! By February she was in the hospital for what I did not know yet. I found out later when someone took me to see her. Actually they snuck me into the hospital since a child had to be 12 to visit. There were IV tubes and monitors hooked up to her. I remember thinking what was going on but didn't ask a lot of questions. Mommy said she had cancer and had a mastectomy. She explained as best she could what it meant. She said the doctors removed her left breast. I was flabbergasted and confused wondering why did they cut off her breast and why only the left one?

My young mind was occupied with what my mother was going through. Cancer invaded my world and I wanted to understand what it was. My thoughts were consumed with: Can I catch it? Where does it come from? Are we born with it? Why does my mother have it? Mastectomy was a new word to me. I learned the spelling of the word so I could find it in the dictionary. It wasn't in there. One day in school I asked my fifth grade teacher to explain cancer. He was in the middle of a totally different subject. He couldn't help me.

When mommy was released from her stay at the hospital I showed her an advertisement in the back of a magazine for a prosthesis breast for women who had a mastectomy. It related to what was happening in ours lives. She told some of her friends of my discovery and my concern like it was very important and special. I felt so responsible and a little grown up knowing I could help her in some way. The prosthesis would make her feel better and all put back together.

Moments.....
that we have -
Memories:
we can share

As the short time mommy had left to live surged on I became more afraid and anxious. All I knew was she was very sick and it was bad. The signs were there. She was crawling on hands and knees from her bedroom to the bathroom moaning in pain. She wouldn't tell me what was wrong with her.

Mommy started talking to me more about things I had no idea about. She wanted to know if she died and came back to see me would I be afraid of her. Did I understand the lyrics to the song "A Rainy Night in Georgia" and do I understand what it was like to be lonely? I never thought about her dying but I would miss her so I told her I would be happy to see her again. She never shared that she was dying.

Death was not something I had ever experienced so I couldn't comprehend what it really was. Children in my day didn't see death and was shielded from it. People who died on TV didn't bleed or cry out in pain. They looked pretty as while they slipped away in glowing lights with beautiful faces.

As the cancer progressed my mother began to hallucinate. I was scared of her by this time. Her behavior was strange and she said what I considered crazy things. I now understand this was probably caused by pain killers and the fact she was dying. By this stage of her illness we moved in with my grandparents. I would talk to my mother from the doorway of her bedroom because I afraid to step into the room. She coaxed me to her one day and gave me three dollars. Mommy took my hand and told me she saw me in a pretty wedding dress and how beautiful I looked. It was the last time I talked to her.

The last day I saw my mother alive she was carried out of the house in the arms of an uncle. They took her to the hospital. I watched the expressions of horror and helplessness on my grandmother's face. She couldn't fix this one with a bandage, a lollipop or chicken soup. She couldn't help her daughter, the second child of four.

Sadly mommy passed away. My father broke the news to my sisters and me with his arms around all of us huddled together on my grandparents little love seat. My daddy had to be joking when I heard him speak those terrible words. But why would he joke about mommy dying? Daddy was so helpless trying his best to get us to understand what he struggled to say. He looked so sad. Daddy searched the room looking for help focusing on my grandfather. My grandfather's head dropped as he mumbled like he was in a trance about arrangements that were made for the wake and the funeral of his baby girl. His voice faded away as I studied everyone and everything in the room. All their faces were filled with sorrow. Then I saw it. There was a photograph of my mother hanging on the wall. It wasn't there before. The photo hung over a white stand holding a book for guest to sign. When my grandfather confirmed what my father said, I knew it was true. My heart seemed to crack then break in half. I broke down and cried. My sisters did the same. Half my heart went with my mother and the other half to my sisters.

My mother's funeral was on March 23rd the day before my 12th birthday. I was supposed to have the birthday party she had planned. There was no happy birthday song just the church choir singing "Oh Happy Day." The cake with

Pamela Delphyne Dees

white frosting was replaced with a white coffin and mommy dressed in all white as were her four little girls. I looked at my mother's face for the last time. She was cold and stiff but looked like sleeping beauty. She had a head full of hair and pretty smooth skin despite going through radiation treatments and medication for pain. For a moment I swore I saw her move. She looked like she was breathing. Yeah, yeah she going to get up I thought. It was all my wishful imagination. My mother will never get up again. She's dead. Why!!!?? Why my mother?

Things were never the same of course. The next day we moved with daddy and his wife, the 5 children from her first marriage and one on the way. My birthday I slept late and woke feeling very tired and down. My siblings tried to catch some birthday licks off me but I didn't want to be bothered. I just sat down and cried. **It was the first day for the rest of my life that I would be a motherless daughter.**

As the days moved onward I played and acted like any other happy and care free 12 year old kid during the day but at night I cried myself to sleep then dreamed about her. I missed my mother so much. Things became worse for me and I felt sick everyday. I missed days in school. Mommy was gone and my life had been changed dramatically. I went from an apartment with a family of 5 to a full house of twelve. It was chaotic. To make matters worse my youngest sister couldn't live with us since she wasn't my father child. She was sent to my mother's parents. I prayed to have my mother back so life would be the way it was before. "Please god!" "Let her come back please!" That was all I wanted and I was convinced she made a mistake by doing this to us.

On occasion we stayed weekends with my grandparents and I was happy to be with my baby sister. My grandfather gave me a ring my mother purchased for my 12th birthday. He finally pulled him self together in August 1971 and took me to size the ring for my finger. We had lunch and he took me to a bar. Most of the patrons there knew my mother. Some of them still seemed sad and missed her. They gave me money when it was revealed I am her daughter. I got to spend time with one of my favorite people in the whole world. It was a very special day. Needless to say tragedy in the form of death came again. My grandfather died in November of 1971 of a heart attack. He may have been grieving my mother and died of a broken heart. My grandfather was my heart. I loved him so.

My life seemed destined to experience nothing but death and my attitude towards life changed. I cared about nothing and hated my life and had low self esteem. No one seemed to care about what I was going through. There was no one to talk to.

I tried to escaped to a world were I hide from all of the craziness. I became anti-social, very quiet and didn't want to be close to anyone. I developed a temper, mood swings and cried easily. I didn't make a many friends because I felt different from everyone else. I just didn't fit in. Pretty much I tried to stay to myself. Not an easy task with 12 people in the house!

I still felt strongly that my mommy had got to come and get me. That she really wanted to come back to her girls and would come soon! I actually packed my clothes and

Pamela Delphyne Dees

89

waited thinking this was nothing but a big mistake on her part. She never came and I slowly got through the terrible grief. Sort of.

My birthday meant nothing much to me for years. The celebration seemed selfish and because my mother's funeral was the day before my birthday I felt god was punishing me. Then it happened. I turned 28. The age my mother died. That is when I realized how short my mother's life was and how little I knew about her. I learned from her friends that her favorite holiday was Christmas, she loved clothes, and the love of her life was not my father! It makes me laugh when I think about that. Especially knowing what I know now about love and men. She was nicknamed Doll by her grandparents because she was so pretty. But as pretty as she was mommy was from the projects and was a tough girl. Momma didn't take no mess from none and could cuss like 10 sailors and fight. Some of her rough and tough I remember and inherited. I love when they talk about their memories of her. I feel closer and understand her better.

The one thing her friends can't give me is the sound of her voice or her laughter. All of those things about her are now a fading memory.

My mother had four girls but always wanted a son. If she was here today the six handsome grandsons, two beautiful grand-daughters, two adorable great-grandsons and a charming little princess of a great-grand daughter would have her heart. She would have been very happy and would spoil all of them especially the boys. Our children will never know her physically but they hear stories and we

Pamela Delphyne Dees

90

A time to reflect -
- thoughts -

have mommy on film from age 16 until shortly before her death. There are photographs and you can see my mother's features in all of her grand and great-grand children. She lives forever through us.

A very dear friend of mine lost her mother in 2005. My heart went out to her because she had years with her mother. Over 40 years. They built a relationship with a strong foundation. I would imagine it kept them strong in their support and love for each other. They could relate to each other as mother to child and woman to woman when it was required. It must have been the greatest feeling to know your mother be it for good or not so good times is there just to talk to. Just for a talk and a hug.

My time with my mother was 11 tiny years. I'll never have what my friends are so lucky to have had with their mothers. No mother daughter talks, sharing, arguments, shopping together, advice, teaching or support. She wasn't there for any of my life changing events like when I became a woman, got my first job, fell in love, had my heart broken, or became a mother.

I am blessed to have my daughter and raised her to have the type of relationship I imagined I would have with my own mother. My daughter and I are very close and she is the "Sunshine of My Life". That's our song. It's the song I sang to her as a baby. Not having my mother probably gave me better insight on being one myself.

It has been 37 years since her passing and I still mourn her, miss her and love her. Sometimes I wonder what type of relationship we would have. My outlook on life grew more positive as years passed but it took a long time. I give honor to my mother and try to live a life she didn't get a chance to. My life is peaceful most days, prosperous and filled with love because that is how I want it. I want to have fun!!! My self esteem has grown. I've learned that life is too short to dwell on the past. We must move on with our lives and live each day with some degree of passion and hope for what is ahead.

I love Mommy.

****

Daddy: One for Daddy-O.

My father's passing is different because I was there for the end. The days leading to his death were scary and full of anxiety. It was rough watching the first man who meant everything, the man who was your first love, the man who helped you tie your shoes and carried you on his shoulders become so frail. My father was diabetic and insulin dependent everyday. The illness took its toll on him since he was diagnosed in 1970's. How old he was when he found out he had it I don't know. I'm guessing late 30's to early forties. Years of dealing with the disease took a toll on his body. His eyesight went bad and he had to have cataract surgery then he had a mild stroke. In 2004 his kidneys began to reach the end stage of renal disease (kidney failure). This made it necessary for him to go on dialysis. He hated it.

Daddy informed us he wanted to get a kidney transplant. He needed to go through a series medical test and psychological evaluation first. My father was adamant not to live the rest of his life on dialysis. He sent out a plea to the family to be tested for possible donors. Some of us were not willing and some not able. I was eligible due to high blood pressure. But daddy persevered and continued with the required medical test. Because this would be an operative procedure one of the required test was a cardio evaluation.

The test revealed daddy had cardiovascular disease. There some blockage in his arteries and surgery was necessary. Now, I will never forget February 14, 2005. Not because it was my daughter's 22nd birthday, no my father decided to have surgery. I got a call to come to Cleveland because his surgery was scheduled for the next morning. In the morning!

Why no discussion first? I can only speculate that he didn't want to be bothered with discussion. Then again I really don't know. My relationship with him was strained until 2 years before this event. Slowly I was working to make it less strained and distant. A lot of incidents contributed to this distance and avoidance after my mother died. All I need to speak on that is he did the best he could with raising 9 children three of which are grieving. We had a blended family and there was some chaos in our home. Everyone did not get along all of the time. Things didn't go the way we wanted sometimes. Both my father and stepmother did the best they could under stressful circumstances. God bless them both.

Daddy was an active man and loved the outdoors. He was born and raised Alabama. He loved to fish and being near water was one of his favorite things to do. He never communicated that but I could see it because every year we would head to the beach. When he and my mother's marriage was no more he come for his visits. I anticipated

Pamela Delphyne Dees

his arrival and when I heard him knock I didn't want to be the one to answer the door. I waited for some else to open the door because I wanted to see him walk in. The sun seemed to glow over his head like a halo and follow him in and stay with him all day. That was a beautiful sight for me to see. The outings I remember most were to the lake. I grew up loving the outside and nature.

Another thing my father loved was music. Weekends at our house were filled with music. Most weekends started off with him playing jazz then Motown and other R&B songs. His taste in music was eclectic from jazz to the Jackson Five and elevator music. He just loved to hear music. Daddy loved to paint. All the paintings in our house were by his hand.

All of that stopped or slowed down when he became diabetic. My sister and I arrived at the hospital around 06:00 after driving all night from Georgia. The surgery was done and Daddy was in the ICU. He looked alert and talking by the time we were able to see him. After a few hours I noticed he started saying he wasn't looking for a job after I told him a friend of mine had a job interview. He was also becoming more and more agitated than normal. Something didn't seem right.

He became combative sometime after that and was tied to his bed. Daddy grew worse. When I left he was still in the same condition. I started doing research on line. The information I found on mortality rates for people with renal disease who had bypass surgery was depressing. The survival rates are low. I prayed. Please help him lord!!

take a moment....

My father stayed in ICU from February to April. He moved to a long term care facility because the hospital could do no more for him. I drove to Ohio to see him from March to June nearly every other week. I was worried. My work hours allowed me to do this because every other week was four days off. Thank god for that.

My father's sister and my oldest step sister took care of him everyday. My step mother was also terribly ill and still recovery from heart surgery due to a heart attack. It was a horrible ordeal for her. She had been hospitalized and on life support but she pulled through. Thank god it was not her time to go.

The time came to face what was evidently my father's fate. My last visit with him was in June. He was declining and needed to come to terms with the possibility he would no longer be with us.

The doctors at the hospital perform a tracheal on him with prevented him to speak or drink water. My father loved water and was very frustrated that he could have any. The days I was there I spoke to him pleading for him to find the will to get better. On the last day I saw him I brought my favorite picture of him playing a guitar and ask if he recognized who it was in the photo. He pointed to his chest. A device was inserted in his throat which allowed him to speak. It was good to hear his voice. I told him I was going to the airport after I leave the facility and he asked why I just got there to see him that day. When I replied that I've been there all week he looked confused. It hurt me to see him that way.

Pamela Delphyne Dees

I let him know I would be back on father's day. Another trip by car racing to get to him on father's Sunday day proved futile. He was admitted the day before to a nursing home because they did all they could at the long term care facility. My plan was to see him the next day but arrived in Ohio too late for visiting hours. In the past my father made it clear that he would never live in a nursing home. On Monday June 20th I got a frantic call from my step sister. She was crying and left a message that daddy was in the hospital. I arrived at the hospital to find him connected to life support. His blood pressure on the monitor was very low. He was already gone but the machines kept him breathing and his heart pumping.

My aunt, step sister and I were there watching and hoping for a change but it was not to be. After a long wait sitting in silence and along discussion with the doctors it was decided to turn off the machines. I called my sisters before we had him disconnected to tell them to come. As soon as the machines were shut off he was dead. I couldn't grasp it. My aunt shook him and a called his name as if she was trying to wake him up. My hear t went out to her. But he was gone. It was June 20th 2005 at 7:15 PM. I will never forget that day. He was 69 years old. We would have been 70 in March the same month I was born.

Memories started flooding my brain and I thanked him for taking care of me after my mother died. For all the fun we had and the love of music he passed down to me. I have my father spirit of love for nature and being free. His death was not as hard as my mother's but it is still hard. I long for my dad because there was so much I still want to know about him. I thank god we got the chance to reconcile and some to an understanding as best we could.

He was hard but I thank him for that. Planning his funeral was hard. We were buried in a brown casket the color of one of his favorite vehicles a Cadillac. His favorite color was brown. He loved cars. Other than the caddy he loved old mustangs.

See I was more prepared for his passing than my mother. I was older and had more life experiences. Only wish I could touch him, hear his voice, watch him walk his stride and tell him that I love him. Many things I don't remember clearly about my mother but I have tons of memories of my daddy.

He was blessed to be able to see his grand children and great grand children. He was always filled with good advice not only for his children but for the other children we grew up with in Cleveland Heights. He was well respected by all of them. One of our high school alumni groups wrote proclamation. On of the lines of that proclamation spoke of how he stood proud in Cleveland Heights when the city was not so kind to African American families. He was one of the pioneers of black families who moved there in the 1960's. They gave him day in his honor. Our friends, mostly men spoke of their memories of my father with love and respect.

My father favorite saying to us was "God Bless the Child Who has That Got His Own". He raised us with that mantra. Daddy left a legacy of how to be friendly. Oh yeah, I called him Daddy-O when I was little cause he told me to. I bought a Cannon Ball Adderly cd with the song "One for Daddy-O" on it. He loved Cannon Ball's music and so do I. Since he had no biological sons he called us boy. (Smile) I really miss him. He was a friendly fun guy who didn't know a stranger.

Pamela Delphyne Dees

I wish he was here. Two years have passed and whenever I hear certain songs I think of him. Lately I have purchased a lot of music he played during those musical weekends the family shared with him. We sang like a female Jackson Five for him. Imitated the Temptations and Supremes. Tried to be little Aretha Franklins all for his amusement..He took me to see the Jackson five when I was 13. He liked the opening at which was the Commodore and proudly announced over and over again that they were from Tuskegee. Introduced me to jazz of every kind when I was a small child, taught me to swim, work on cars, appreciate art and be a handy lady to take of minor repairs in my own home. He was good at fixing things in the house. I can do that too.

His dying gave me more enthusiasm for life. To go out and try to fulfill my desires and dreams. There is a big empty space left in my life without him. Still I wish he was here.

I love Daddy!
Pamela Delphyne Dees

moving on

This dying thing has been a really trying thing not that I'm different from anybody else, but it has really torn me apart. The first major death for me was my Grandfather Orrin L. Tolliver Sr. I was 5 and disliked my father, so he was my savior and he kept me safe from his ignorance. At the time I was 6 going on 7, so life moved on.

The next major hit for me was losing my MOM she was my best friend and the greatest Mother ever. We didn't have a lot but she made sure we had what we needed. I saw my Mother go through so much stress being a single Mom and still being in love with an evil motherf--ka. The question is does God make mistakes? Please forgive me because in his case he dropped the ball.

David Louis Tolliver

As I get older my Sister and I wonder why God didn't take him instead of my Mother. That was 1990 and that year was a tough one starting on the first day of the year my next door neighbor Mr. Harris died from a long battle with Cancer. My Grandmother kept getting on me to go see him and when I finally did he was dying right in front of my face.

Then Mother's Day my Great-Grandmother Georgia Beard died from a long battle with Alzheimer's. You want to talk about a fantastic cook man, on the holidays alone she would prepare a feast fit for 100 people and the whole family would come by and have a ball. That's what family is all about. I lived Soul Food. Then on August 2nd three days after my 20th birthday it happened.

David Louis Tolliver

103

Back then I worked overnights at WZAK in Cleveland. When I got off I went home and went straight to bed and dreamed my Mom had died! This is crazy when I woke up it felt like somebody slapped the sh-t out of me the phone rang and my Mom's friend was on the phone frantic, "your Mother passed out at the wheel and they rushed her to St. Alexis hospital.

When I arrived she was dead ICE COLD and I ran as fast as I could. I will never forget that day as long as I live. The crazy thing is in the years to follow a lot of things in my memory blacked out and I can't remember a lot from then. Anyway at this point I stopped believing in God until My singing partner Jason champion and Fred Graves brought me back.

David Louis Tolliver

the remedy of nature

(Cousins) Orrin III, David L (center) & David "DèTyme" TOLLIVER

after the funeral for
Frances Edith Nix Tolliver
in the basement of
St Paul A.M.E. Zion Church on 55th & Quincy in Cleveland, O.

Well the years went by and I wasn't affected by death until Biggie and Tupac were killed. At this point I was like damn these cats are my age and I was supposed to be at the party that Big got killed at. WHOA! In my mind I knew we all have to go but damn my Mom was 38 so that scared the hell out of me. I started having panic attacks and was scared to death of dying.

My friend Carlton Williams and I both went through the same sh-t he literally had to drop out of school to take care of his Grandma, who slowly died of Cancer. Well time moved on and here we are November 10th, 2006 and I'm in Cleveland, Ohio to sing at a funeral for my friends Mom the next day.

While leaving the Airport to get my friend Theresa

some Krispy Kreme doughnuts I get the most shocking phone call of my life. My good friend Ronnie Knight called me and said, "Hey Dave did Gerald die?" I said, "Man get the f--out of here let me call you back." As soon as I hung up Joe Little of the Rude Boys called me crying like a baby and said,"Dave, Gerald is gone"! It was as if somebody slapped the sh-t out of me again. I couldn't even cry I was in shock. He was only 40.

This man was responsible for my music career and wrote the song that kept me paid. On top of that the song" So Alone was a song he wrote for me to sing in memory of my Mother, Then 13 years later having to honor his life with it. Though we had our share of issues most being a young entertainer not knowing the business feeling myself I went after him.

To make a long story short we patched things up but it wasn't the same but we were cool. We even did business again and it seemed as if he were somewhere, I was there too. So you know me I went to all the shows, one because I knew he might call me out to sing with him and those times were some of the best of my life. Then it happened again some worthless broad tried to get us to go at it again and I'm glad we worked it out. This broad was a stalker and she thought by working with Men At Large or Gerald's sister it would get her closer to him, NOT! In the end him and I laughed about it and I looked him in the eye and said," Man I love you and I miss you and I want us to start working together again".

This was a sign and a lot of times we don't see the signs. Before this time I saw Gerald at his birthday celebration and he looked very tired and bigger than normal. The next time I saw him was October 19th, 2006 in Birmingham, Ala. That's when I told him how I felt. Three weeks later I lost my Brother, my Friend, my Teacher and the greatest entertainer of all-time. This has torn me apart and I cry inside daily because of my love and admiration of this man. I am thankful to Eddie and Martha for their Son and for letting me be a part of your family's legacy.

Well I know it seems as if I'm writing a book but this is therapy. I'm glad I had this opportunity to vent. My final chapter is about the greatest woman to ever walk this earth Frances Edith Nix Tolliver a.k.a. Franny B.

nature is one of God's medicines

My Grandmother took care of us from beginning until she had to be confined to a nursing home. Here is the, conclusion this woman was a devout, dedicated, God-fearing woman you could kick her -ss and the next day she would give you the shirt off her back. She didn't have a terminal disease but she might as well have. By the end of her life she couldn't talk, move, eat, or clean herself without assistance.

She was a proud woman and I know she didn't want anyone to see her like this. So my question is this, for a woman who was so loving and faithful to God why did she have to suffer for such a long time? We have always been taught or forced as kids to believe if; you question God something bad would happen.

David Louis Tolliver

Well I know she didn't question God and I know she was faithful, at least when I was around. So somebody tell me and I don't want to hear the typical clichés. Unless she was a serial killer or a child molester she didn't deserve to live her last days like this. At this stage of my life now I have my own views my Sister Verdelle says I'm angry well you know what, I am.

So I am going to live the rest of my days to please me, whatever that may be. As long as I take care of my family and don't out right hurt nobody I DON'T GIVE A F--K!

David Tolliver

Men At Large

I will never forget the last time I saw my Father (Nicholas). In life he was a very strong man who worked as a bridge painter, he was a great provider and a wonderful husband to my Mother.

In the fall of 1982 he suffered a massive stroke which left him paralyzed on his left side.
This was devastating to our family especially to my Mother who had a special place for my Father in her heart.

My Father was introduced to my Mother in 1945 after the World War. In 1946 my Mother found out she had (T.B) tuberculosis, everyone knew she could die. My Father fell in love with her and willed her to live, as she had given up living feeling she was going to die. She had no insurance or medical plan, only having been in this country a short time arriving from Greece.

My Father fresh out of the Army and with his new bridge painting job knew he was going to marry this woman; he loved her and was determined to help her. He went to the hospital everyday until she got better. He paid for all her medical bills from his bridge painting job and eventually after all the surgery she recovered and they got married.

He was doing all this while his Mother my Grandmother was ill in Greece, he sent what he could to Greece to help his mother who eventually passed in 1957.

My parents had a great life together until my Father passed away on January 12th 1991.
We had the Funeral and laid him to rest on the morning of January 16th 1991.

My wife Kathy who was pregnant at the time started having labor pains soon after the funeral; we rushed her to the Hospital where she gave birth to our son Nicholas on the morning of January 18th 1991.
At the time I was feeling all kinds of emotions.
One this is certain though my Faith in God and Jesus became much stronger.

And now as of this writing, I am praying everyday in hopes of being able to see my Mother live one more day, she is now 90 years old and in very poor health. We are all there for her just like my Father was, including her Grandson Nicholas.

The last words my Father spoke to me was, Son keep the Faith.

Chris Mavros

a kiss....
from the lips of nature

JANUARY THE 29TH

It was one dark, lonely dreary day.
God decided to take my sweet momma away.

This is a day I will never forget.
When I lie down and dream about it
I awaken in a cold sweat.

Why is the pain always so great?
This is everyone's destiny and everyone's fate.

The day my mother died,
I never wanted to leave her side.
I just stood there and I cried and I cried.

My sisters were there with the whole family.
We tried to waken her but she slept so peacefully.

I was talking to my mother and I asked her a question.
I asked her how I could make her more comfortable
It was only a suggestion.

Seems like she shrugged up her shoulder!
I just wanted to grab her and hold her.

The nurse came to tell us
that her breathing was really low.
That's when she told us
I think it's time for your mother to go.

One day before she left,
she asked my cousin was she going home today?
Right then and there
my sister read her bible and started to pray.

The promise momma made to me
she certainly did keep
She said that I would miss her again I began to weep.

Now it's here again, January the 29TH

©Janet Marie Sorey Lochard 3/2006

What I have learned from the death of my Mother and Father is that it is final. Any belief in the hereafter is fine, but as for your life on earth, death is final.

So you had better take advantage of the time that you have with your parents to love them and be with them and speak with them as much as possible, because you will sure miss those opportunities when they are gone. So if there is a heaven, then you will be able to meet with them when you get there, but if not you goofed.

John Fagot

Sonny Jones 1938-1988

Growing up, my daddy was my life.

He encouraged me to be all I could be, he is the reason for my career in the music industry and he is the reason I became the woman I am. Don't get me wrong, I absolutely adore my beautiful mother and she is still a major part of my life it's just that I was "the" daddy's girl.

I never thought he would die.

My daddy was a rolling stone to say the least in the early 70's but in the early 80's he gave his life to Jesus Christ. Boy did he change. No more dirty jokes! He loved the Lord with an incredible passion, something that I couldn't relate to *back then*.
When he got sick with a very rare condition, I worried that he would "leave me" but he always said he couldn't until I was saved...I vowed then and there that I would never be saved if it meant I couldn't have him anymore...

Well, he did leave me and I thought I would surely die, I wanted to die.

Because of our closeness, I knew the exact time he went into the coma, I felt it in my soul, I knew he wanted me to go home (back to Atlanta) because he knew I couldn't handle watching him die, and I knew when he wasn't going to make it another night because I again "felt him" and I knew the exact time he died. I believe that he "passed" through on his way to glory that night, that's how I knew to answer my sisters call at 3:09am with "he's gone isn't he?" She wondered how I knew and I said because he came to say goodbye. I cried and begged GOD to let me kiss him one more time...there were many times I picked up the phone to call him forgetting he was gone. I was angry for a long time until someone said to me that your dad loved Jesus in a mighty way and have you ever stopped to think more about how happy he is than about how sad you are?

Wow. No I hadn't, I just selfishly wanted him here. I know that all my daddy wanted was to be with Jesus and I know that he is...it took 10 long years for me to "feel better" and accept that he didn't "leave me", he is in a much better place.

The good news is that, I now know that incredible love my daddy used to always talk about. It swells my heart because I know he is so happy that now "Jesus is my life".

PJ Jones

Warner Bros. Records
Urban Promotions

When I was 11 yrs old, I learned about the word "Dying" first hand. I lost my youngest brother who at age 9, died from Leukemia. He was diagnosed with this cancer at the age of 4 yrs old. I knew he was sick but not that sick that he was going to die. In the midst of his sickness, I gave him the best last years of his life. I was his big sister and I had to be just that. On the night before he died, I remember hearing some yelling, screaming and crying. My father whose only son, was dying in his bed.

That was so devastating that it woke everyone up in the house. As I approached down the stair steps, I was stopped by my Mother. She told me go back upstairs with tears in her eyes. That's when I knew the time had come, for my brother to go to heaven. Before I went back upstairs, I saw my Father down on his knees, praying with at least 3-4 bibles and pleading for GOD not to take his son. He had the room lit with candles as well.

I ran so fast upstairs to my room and just cried so hard under my covers in bed. My brother passed 3 days later on May 4, 1978. My Mom was with him when he passed in Rainbow Babies and Children's Hospital in Cleveland Ohio. Although I didn't get a chance to say goodbye, my Mother said he passed very peacefully. To me, I was not at peace like everyone else. I would still look for him in his bed everyday I woke up in the morning and before I go to bed.

It was so hard for me to accept that my best friend was gone. He was my rock and my brother to the end.

L.L. Bryant

The very close bond that we shared, I felt it was taken away. I didn't understand why GOD chose him to be his angel. He was only 9 years old, so lovable, so intelligent and so precious. I had asked everyone, "Why did GOD have to take my brother away. He didn't do anything to anyone. Why couldn't he take someone else?" That is an answer that today, I still do not understand on why so many good people have passed on to another place.

Then the day before my brother had passed, my great uncle died in the nursing home. That was hard on my great aunt, who I called "Granny." You see, when my Grandmother had passed, my mom was just 4 years old and 9 children had been left without parents in the home. My grandfather had passed before my grandmother and someone had to take on the children. My great aunt and uncle, helped with the raising. I knew him well by visiting him every Saturday with Granny but didn't know he was that sick either.

So we had 2 funerals within 3 weeks and it devastated the whole entire family. So imagine; on May 3, 1978, you get a call stating that a loved one had passed. You are dealing with that with family and friends. Then on the next day, you get another phone call stating that another loved one had passed. Wow! The Williams/Bryant family was in deep grieving.

L.L. Bryant

During all this bereavement, I had a best friend named Angela. She was my true best friend and sister through Christ. We grew up on the same street as infants and until we graduated from high school. She was my best friend in the whole wide world and no one could ever take that away from me. On May 14, 1991, she had called me and asked if I wanted to hang out. I accepted and she came and picked me up from my apartment. She was married, with 2 children (twin boy and girl) and we went for a ride.

As we pulled up to a deli store, she put the car in park and turned to me. She stated that her marriage was on the rocks, the baby boy can't come home from the hospital due to still being in a ventilator since birth and baby girl is a busy, busy toddler. She is in school and working a part-time job to maintain the home. She stated to me that she was so tired but knew she couldn't give up her dreams. Dreams of graduating from college, leaving her husband and being a single parent and living in a beautiful house. Angie had dreams and she was going to live them out.

On May, 16, 1991, she called me and told me that she was leaving her husband for good. Although she told me why, I advised her to do what she thinks is best for her mind, body and soul. She then arrived at her sister's house and unpacked. Sadly, the next following morning, she was giving her self a nebulizer breathing treatments and something went wrong. Per her sister, she was unable to breath, told her sister that she was dying and passed out onto the floor.

L.L. Bryant

has someone died on you, and sometime
after, you think about calling them, or
going over to their house, then realize....
that they're gone.... for good?

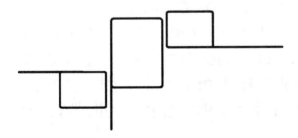

Angie was rushed to a nearby hospital and died on the way. They were unable to revive her and it was over. I could not believe that "Death" had taken someone so close away from me again. I was devastated from the time I received the call until I left the hospital that morning. I could not believe that my best friend for life was gone. I kept trying to wake her up on that gurney in the ER and she did not wake up. I screamed and hollered her name and begged her not to leave me like this. She was gone.

Why did GOD do this to me again? I was so mad at myself because I told her to do what she thought was best in her marriage. I blamed myself for not calling her that morning to see what her plans were for Mothers day. GOD called her home on Mothers Day and it shocked the whole family. Instead of getting dressed for church, we had to get her dressed for a funeral. I lost another best friend.....again

As the days went by, I was scared to get close to anyone and it made me become so depressed. I stopped going to church and turned my depression toward drugs and alcohol. At this point, I didn't care about nothing. I suppressed it all knowing that I had to understand this thing called, "Death," before I could accept it. What is the purpose of being born if we are going to die?

I was really afraid that sooner or later, everyone around me was going to die at any minute. Then in 1992, I lost my cousin who died in her house. My mom was the last person who spoke to her on the phone 2 days before she was found. I thought to myself, "What

L.L. Bryant

the hell is going on?" Why is it again, that people who have been so close to me are dying. I thought that this was crazy. This thing called, DEATH" is serious! Then two months later, a guy that I was dating, was murdered. My heart was so torn and I felt trapped in my surroundings. Well by August of 1992, I decided to move out of Ohio and moved to Delaware with my oldest sister.

I had to get away because I could not take it anymore. Once I had relocated, I felt a sense of relief and my fears began to calm down. I had to make some adjustments on the new jobs, but I was very private and really didn't make friends right away. I felt at peace with myself and no one could take that away from me.

Then in 1993, I got a call that my other cousin (whose sister had died the previous year) had passed away. Since I was not there in Ohio, the feeling was acceptable and I had no serious fears. It was so sad that 2 sisters had died within a year of each other. Then in 1994, both of the sisters who had passed, their father passed. I felt the fear but it was a calm fear of "It's OK". A few more friends and relatives have passed but, I have accepted it a little better.

My biggest fear is losing my parents in the near future and actually learning on how to deal with it. Being in therapy to this day, I still have to cope with Life and Death. It's not a subject that I like to chit-chat about.

L.L. Bryant

Meanwhile, I just enjoy everyday that GOD has granted me another day and I pray that he has blessed my family and close friends with the same blessings. So never let a day go by without calling them or visiting them in person.

This thing called "Death" is a serious situation. No one is prepared even if you know it is going to happen eventually. So I decided to sit back and evaluate some thoughts. I read that:

"Life is pleasant. Death is peaceful. It's the transition that's troublesome

What is there to do when people die, people so dear and rare, but bring them back by remembering

Life is a preparation for the future; and the best preparation for the future is to live life as if there were none

By L.L. Bryant
4/18/2007

March 17, 2000- Alberta, my grandmother who raized me, becomez deathly ill and confined to a bed barely talking; fed by a tube

March 10, 2004- Sentwali YaYa, my son, diez

March 01, 2005- Pain, my majestic rottie and companion of 7 yearz, diez

March 09, 2007- Alberta, my grandmother who raized me, diez

March 19, 2007- Zari, the cat that we acquired az a kitten after Sentwali died, to still add new life to the family, found dead in my yard.

Grandmother waz a strong one
in 2000 the doctorz said she waz done
Told ma mother
tell the family to come on
so we could be by her bedside when she died
Soon az I got the call I left work, jus like that
doin' 95 on the Howard Franklin, thinkin' back
to when I waz afraid of the dark
and would wake ma grandmother with late nite knocks
And this matriarch, understandin' ma fearz, would let
me in
to sleep next to her, tho ma mother told her not to
Guess she loved me so much she had to
I know she loved me so much she waz glad to

get up at 5:30 every mornin',
from ma first day of kindergarten to the day I
graduated
to make sure I had a hot meal before school
And I can still smell the food
still hear the hymnz she'd be in the kitchen hummin'
lettin' me know the gritz waz comin'
Still hear her talkin' to the characterz on her favorite tv
showz
still see her wigglin' her toez- day and night
And theze vizionz compared with the image of her
motionless and bedridden
are like the difference between day and nite
It waz hard
Watchin' ma mother struggle with ma
grandmother waz even harder

But ma mother'z a strong one
round the clock, she'd be feedin' her, flippin' her, turnin her
comin' up with homemade remediez to make sure
grandmother'z bed sorez stopped burnin' her
Despite what waz ailin' or hurtin' her,
for 7 yearz ma mother waz a miracle worker
But this year, on March 9, it ended
Guess grandma had given all she had till she waz tired
of givin' and decided
it waz finished
While I'll miss her every minute
I'm glad she'z restin' finally
And
although I'm no longer afraid of the dark
I'll alwayz remember her az the light that showed me
it waz alright to be

www.lifeizpoetry.com myspace.com/lifeizpoetry

We The Living

Written by **Rhonda Anderson**
Circa 1994 – as a reflection on my feelings about death
after my grandparents had passed

Oh death, where is thy sting?
Come drape me with your gloomy cloak
Let me find peace at last
As my final words are spoke

My eyes begin to grow heavy
My heart beat begins to slow
An eerie calmness overtakes me
A feeling we the living do not know

We arrive in to this world
Ignorant of life's wondrous display
Sad to say so many of us
Will leave exactly the same way

People will come into our lives
To love, enlighten and inspire
Yet we often don't express our true feelings
Until after a person has expired

Daily death taunts us all
With biddings to shorten our time
Plane crashes, car wrecks, cigars and cigarettes
Suicide, drugs, alcohol and crime

Still daily we live on in our complacent modes
Futilely ignoring the reality
That if we don't stop and really start living this life
We the living one day will not be

Rhonda Anderson　　　　－ Circa 1994 －

Well, I've read almost everybody's passages and words of experiences. I am going to deviate a little from the norm with what I'm about to write as I've experienced many, many deaths from beloved human beings that have entered my soul. From family members, friends and even certain legends that me and my group(Full Force) have worked with such as James Brown & Gerald Levert.

Those are the human beings that have had certain various effects on me when they've died. It's so funny that even though we all know that we as well as every human being has to die sometimes, the majority of us still find it hard to accept. Well...I want to reflect on 2 pets that me and my family once had. 2 Dogs...one was a little German Sheppard named Apollo. (Named after me and my brother's triumphant experiences of performing at the Apollo back in the 70's and the other a Collie/German Sheppard named Tuna.

Both dogs though not human beings, were like humans to us. They were part of our living breathing family and we loved them just like we'd love a family member. (I'm sure many of u can relate) We had Apollo for 5 years. (I have a playful bite mark imprint to remind me of him) & our other dog Tuna was a part of our family for 17 years. We loved them so, so, so much. And even though they never spoke back to us in human English...they both understood our English language when we directed it to them.

Now with Apollo, as much as we all loved him, he was a terror full of mischief. Whenever any of us would try to remove his collar to give him a bath, it would be a battle; he loved to bite, even in playing.

Bowlegged Lou/Full Force

It would be intended love bites but some of those damned bites would sink in as real bites. Thank God he never had rabies. No one could ever take off his collar except my uncle Nelson. Apollo obeyed and respected Uncle Nelson. Apollo's crazy vice was he loved, loved going outside to take his walk. He just loved going outside. Every time he knew he was going outside....he would start panting with excitement all over the place. It was like he was having an orgasm.

When Apollo died after 5 years of having him, it was a sad sad sad state in our family house with my 2 brothers (Paul Anthony and B-Fine) and my mom and dad. One night, I took Apollo over to my grandmother's house where my aunt and cousin were visiting. (They all loved Apollo.) But dumb me; while in my grandmother's living room, I gave Apollo's leash to my young 5 yr old cousin to hold onto cause she wanted to play with Apollo in the house....but while holding onto the leash....Apollo's supersonic ears heard the opening of the downstairs door as my aunt was coming inside.

Apollo who of course loves to go outside started heading for the downstairs door while dragging my lil' cousin along. She let go of the leash...Apollo dashed downstairs....I followed with the quickness trying to grab back onto the leash....but Apollo scooted down so fast and darted straight outside in the street as my aunt opened the door. I saw with my young eyes, our dog Apollo get run over by a car.

Bowlegged Lou/Full Force

I fell to the ground and started crying because he never got up. My uncle Nelson who was with his friends across the street was the one to pick up Apollo from the street and carry his 'boy'. Maaaan, I'm getting a little emotional right now as I reflect on this. Anyway my whole family was filled with emotion as everyone just started crying when they found out about Apollo. Crazy, huh?? I bet some of u readers never counted pets/animals as friends or family members that can be a part of this book (This Dying Thing) huh??

As far as our other dog Tuna who my dad found on the street.......She was with us for 17 years and she was human to us. Ha ha! Tuna was the daughter my mom never had because that's how she treated her. My mom talked to Tuna everyday and all family members knew that Tuna was my mom's 4 legged daughter. Whenever Tuna got sick....my mom would give her actual human medicine and she would always, always put vitamins in Tuna's food. She would break open the capsule and let the liquid vitamin juice seep out into Tuna's bowl of food.

Tuna was a family staple of 17 years and as she got older,,,, she was starting to lose her sight.....she couldn't go up and down the steps anymore. We literally had to lift her in our arms and carry her up and down the stairs. Is that love or what?? They say a dog is man's best friend but also a dog can be a family's best friend too.

I remember we had to put Tuna to sleep because she was dying of ailments and old age. I remember seeing her for the last time b4 she went to the ASPCA hospital.

Bowlegged Lou/Full Force

I knew that would be the last I saw her. My mom and my brother took Tuna to the hospital. It was devastating to my mom but it was something that had to be done to eliminate Tuna's suffering.   So u see....beloved pets that stay with u for a long time automatically becomes a life force for your heart as well. When they die, a part of u die too. Same hurt sometimes, same emotions. Though a dog is not a human being, they are still a living breathing component that u become attached to, when they become a staple of your family or a staple of bondship. Apollo and Tuna....two 4-legged examples of emotional feelings and mourning when they became the feature scenario regarding "that dying thing".

A message to the readers.....Never take anyone, anything or anybody for granted. Life is so short and u don't ever know what day is your last. Take time out to say I love u to a loved one. Don't wait for a special occasion.   I would appreciate if u guys check out our myspace site.....WWW.Myspace.com/FullForce and www..ForcefulWorld.com. Check out a single that we have out on a cd from Sony Records entitled Full Force/Legendary. There is a song called "Everyday Is Mother's Day" on it. As well as u can purchase it from itunes as well. We shouldn't ever have to wait for a Sunday in May to wish or show our mother some love.

Bowlegged Lou/Full Force

Bowlegged Lou
(with the cap on, holding Ashanti)

Whether your mom is here on earth with you or up in heaven with the almighty......
EVERYDAY IS MOTHER'S DAY.

Stay Blessed Everybody and may all the positive and optimistic things in life forever be yours.

BOWLEGGED LOU OF FULL FORCE.

OVER THE COURSE OF MY LIFETIME

Over the course of my lifetime, 45 years, I have experienced many losses. With each loss, I search for the lesson within. The losses of my aunt and grandmother have taught me some of my favorite lessons; savor life and keep the faith.

When I was 20 years old, my aunt, Nitsa, was dying of cancer. She was 42 years young. To me she was my dear aunt, my elder. To the world, Nitsa was a young mother, in the prime of her life. Her words of advice; enjoy life, live life to the fullest. She recommended love, and laughter. She urged me to make adventure as important as work. Nitsa told me that when someone invites me to do something, or to go somewhere, I should answer yes. I should welcome and embrace the opportunity. I must remember that life is precious.

In 1990, my beloved Grandmother, Yiayia, passed over in my presence. Marigo was born in Greece in the early 1900's. She was a woman of faith and hope. She regaled me with stories from the Bible. Each day was a day to teach me of the saints and their miracles. Yiayia was adored by many; she had a kind and loving heart.

The day of her death was her last lesson to me about faith. On her last day of life on earth, she lay in a hospital bed, unresponsive to nurses, doctors and family. I kept her company and talked to her. It was a cold and sunny December day. I prayed for her recovery. In the alternative, I prayed that if God needed to call her home that he do so quickly and gently. Within the hour, Yiayia was called home. For the first time in two days, she opened her eyes, and looked up towards the ceiling. She extended her arms in prayer, the same way I had seen her pray so many times before. Yiayia smiled, her eyes were wide open. She looked so content. She breathed her last breath and the machines that monitored her life sounded.

It was my honor and privilege to experience this moment with her. Watching her pass over has made me less afraid to die. Yiayia departed this life for another, she went on a journey, and she went home to God.

Live a life of faith and hope. Maintain a kind and loving heart. Seek peace. Embrace adventure, enjoy the journey. Thank you for allowing me to share some of my journey.

Donna Zapis-Thomas

This thing we call "Life and Death". As a little girl I remember spending an enormous amount of time over my maternal grandparent's house. Fred and Fannie Beachum, both born in Mississippi, migrated to Cleveland, Ohio during the 1950's. My grandfather, Fred Beachum was a carpenter, and Fannie was a house wife, that didn't want for anything. Fred worked several jobs to make sure his two kids had everything, and that his wife didn't have to work at all.

Somewhere around 1980 Fred took ill. Fannie spent her every moment taking care of Fred. Fannie took Fred from doctor to doctor, spending countless hours at the Cleveland VA Hospital. Over the course of four or five years Fred had several strokes and several ailments that continuously took over different parts of his body. I watched and contributed to helping in any way to take care of my grandfather. After so many years of Fred suffering, and Fannie trying everything from doctors to trying Ernest Ansley's healing power. Fred's fight ended April 4, 1984. With the back and forth of Fred's health every one was actually prepared for his passing.

After Fred passed Fannie did several things that Fred always wanted to do for her. Fannie was always a family person that spent much of her time with her grandchildren, and siblings. Fannie really started to surround herself around her kids and grandkids. I

Michelle Tolliver

143

remember playing dress up with Fannie in her clothes. I also remember roller skating with Fannie in her basement, and traveling to spend time with her family. Grandma Fannie spent so much time with us that she was looking at buying a bike and signing up to take roller skating lessons.

In Cleveland, Ohio in the 80's kids went back to school from summer vacation after Labor Day. Fannie's family the McDonald McClain Family always held their family reunion during Labor Day. The Labor day of 1984 Grandma Fannie, my mom Gwen, my brother Kevin, and I went to Hernando, Mississippi for our family reunion. During the family reunion Fannie had the time of her life. Fannie made sure she spent true quality time with her mother "Big Momma", her remaining siblings, nieces and nephews. Finding out a year later; during this family reunion Fannie had a conversation with Big Momma. Big Momma told Fannie that she would come spend Christmas or Thanksgiving with her. Well Fannie replied to her mother, "No! Ma, I'm going home, and you won't see me anymore". "The kids are starting back to school, and I don't know what I am going to do with Kevin and Michelle back at school".

Fannie was very lonely with Fred being gone, and she had never been left alone before. One week after school started, on a Sunday night after sitting with my Grandma in church earlier. Fred came back on Lotus Drive in Cleveland, Ohio to get my Grandma Fannie.

Michelle Tolliver

Fred didn't want Fannie to be scared or lonely. Fannie was 57 years young, and went home to be with her husband just 5 months after he passed away.

Fannie was found with her sheets clinched in her hands, pulled up to her face, as if she had seen a ghost. No ghost, just Fred, coming to get his pride and joy. Fannie and Fred also took their brand new Lincoln Mark V for one last spin. During Fannie's home going services their new Lincoln wouldn't start. We just figured they were joy riding around heaven for a few days. Soon as the services were over and out of town family was gone; the car started.

Several years after Fannie and Fred, my other grandmother Gladys Marie Allen passed away, after being ill and suffering for years. Every death that I have experienced through, I can honestly say I understand. I was raised to know that "Everything Happens for a Reason", whether we know the reason or not. Only being 10 years old and dealing with the death of my Grandma Fannie. My Grandma Fannie was everything to me, and I am so thankful for spending so much time with her, and able to remember so much about her, along with the many lessons she shared with me. I was extremely hurt that she was gone, but as I got older and heard Big Momma's story about their conversation, and listening to my very strong mother, I understand. I also understand why my Grandma Marie passed in 1992, and a lady I could consider my Godmother Robin Addie in 2004.

Michelle Tolliver

Death is something that affects everyone differently, and that we can't ever be completely prepared for, however, I UNDERSTAND! There is something to be gained from everyone's death that we all need to UNDERSTAND!

Michelle Tolliver

Death is the beginning of the end. If you are a religious person, you believe in heaven and hell. That being said, the end will last forever. We should take death as a learning experience and motivation. Better ourselves so that when we pass the ones who love us, who remain, can live on. Maybe they too will learn as I did.

Orrin Tolliver III

Orrin (age 8) looking back, David (age 6) behind the desk

LAST MAN STANDING

This Crimson Aura Emitted
The Atmosphere of Death is Here
Millions Have Lost Their Lives Today,
But I Am The Last Man Standing

The Sights, The Struggle, The Adrenaline Pumping
The Pain, The Perseverance...

Knowing That I Must Live One
Because Motivation is the Motif of My Mind Frame
I Cannot Die Today;
Too Much of My Life is Yet to be Lived
I know I have Too Much to Give
This World, it Needs me Because Most Human Beings
Lack Guidance
So In Compliance With that Knowledge, I also know
That death is Not an Option

I've Seen the Light, and Turned Away
Escaped the Band Wagon of Death Today
and Despite the Trauma and Physical Endure
I Am The Last Man Standing

Death, Be Not Proud For I Do Not Fear Thee
Just Merely Escaped Your Wave Again
I've Lost Too Many Friends to You
Family, Too
And One Day, I'll Avenge Them
But, Life is to be Cherished
Even Though it Seems Unfair, A Good Life is Rare
But a *Full* Life is Even Rarer...

I've Seen in My Lifetime Masses of Men
March to Their Demise
And I Along Side Them March at Their Pace
Yet, I'm the Only to Survive
And at Times I'd Try to Lay With Them
But I Must be the Insomniac of Eternal Rest
So I Lay to Wake Again
Death, Be Not Proud For I Do Not Fear Thee
Just Merely Escaped Your Wave Again

It's All Around Me
My Sanity Dwindling
Gangrene, Ignorance, and Poverty Dwelling
Humanity's Quelling While
This Crimson Aura is Steady Swelling

Centuries Pass
Billions of Human Beings are Now Gone Before Me
And I *Still* Am The Last Man Standing

Every Generations I've Watched Martyrs Get Murdered
For The Same Causes I've Supported
Getting Caught Up in My Eternal Existence is The Only
Thing Which Grayed My Hair
I Don't Even Fatigue, The Tears Which Roll Down My
Cheeks Are The Only Things That Bag My Eyes
Too Many Times At Night I've Cried, I Pour Waterfalls
Inside My Heart
I've Been Around Since The Dawn Of Time And A
Glimpse Of *Death* Is All I've Caught

David "DéTyme" Poet Tolliver

149

By My Side, The Mighty Have Fallen. *The Sickest Sights A Man Can Witness*
Civilizations Lay To Waste While The Cracks Of My Toes Taste Their Fermentation
Millenniums Pass In The Blink Of An Eye and I Still Stand In Stagnation

More Consistent than the Cycle of the Sun
Pain and My Heart are Now Bound As One
There's No Eclipse on My Existence, Persistently
Multitudes Continuously Collapse
As I Am The Last Man Standing

I Hate to See The World Stop For Me as I Walk Stagnate
Oceans of Blood For The Fallen
I Despise That My Demise is Implausible
I am the Cause, the Effect and the Absence of Resolution
The Action, Reaction and the Unknown Spirit of Revolution
My Being Has No Conclusion.
I Feel Like The Ghost of Gettysburg, The Phantom of Forever and The Spirit of Nine Eleven

In the War for Immortality,
The Victory of Living I Rejoice Alone
See I'd Happily Exceed My Death in a Heartbeat, For I've Had My Fair Share
My Own and Many Others,
For at Their Last Beat I Was There

David "DéTyme" Poet Tolliver

Their Last Breath, Last Utterance, I've Even Shared Their
Last Stare
And Every Time Another Passes I'll be Watching as They
Gasp For Air

Eternity Is a Long Time... Until You Realized That You've
Lived It Twice
Time Makes You Grow Cold, When Mixed With What
I've Seen In Life
To The Point Where I Can't Even Cry... When I Stare Into
Your Eyes... *And Watch You Die*...
Oh Yeah, And Down The Line... When Your Time Is Up...
You Should Feel My Presence...

I'll Be The Last Man Standing By Your Side

David "DéTyme" Poet Tolliver

when my sister died in '90 - my sons -
Orrin III & David, helped me deal with the grief
just by them being alive.
they didn't say anything
they didn't do anything any different....
they were just around me, and that was comfort.
they were 5 and 3 at the time...

My experience with the Death of my mother:

Well I must begin with my meaning of Death, to me death is the final stage of a persons life, some in the church may say death is the doorway to eternal life, just the thought of death still make tears come to my eyes knowing one day I will not be here to share in my kids life. I know God and the bible teaches us not to be afraid, but when I really have those quiet moments the fear does take over.

The death of my mother, my friend, a person I could share anything with, my home made babysitter, the person who still cooked for me even in my 30's. I could go to her house and stay as long as I wanted to without someone saying, go where you pay rent. My mother's death was sudden we had no time to prepare. It was 3:00am in the morning I get a call that the ambulance had been called my mother could not breath, she was having problems just catching her breath, I arrived at her place the ambulance was already there, she was telling them that she was having problems breathing they gave her oxygen to see if this would help, but it did not, they transported her to the hospital, my mother died in the ambulance on the way to the hospital. I never got the chance to say goodbye or I love you mom. When we finally arrived at the hospital we were escorted into this room, it was called the quiet room, there was a priest waiting for us, all I could say to myself was this is not good, he told us what happened my mother had a heart attack in the ambulance, they tried to revive her, but the attempt was unsuccessful.

This happened almost 9 years ago, and I remember it like it was yesterday, it seems like the entire world just stopped, and I could not function for about 3 weeks. Each day is another day of growing and accepting what has happened, I sometimes wonder why, questioned GOD as to why my mother, because as a young woman I still needed her guidance in my life. My mother was a single parent most of her life, so she always took care of us like mother and father, did not spare the rod, trained us to be young ladies always respecting ourselves I thank her for the things she instilled in me. Death is not easy to cope with, it's a daily process that you as the person must go through, and sometimes it's unexpected.

Connie Melton

Death really touched my heart when I lost my mom in March of 1988. Until then I was able to adjust to losing others that were close to me even though I missed them. But my mom was the first love I ever knew. I remember going to the hospital in her last hours and saying goodbye.

I left St. Lukes hospital and never went back there. I was devastated beyond belief. I remember my son's godmother saying this will make you a stronger person. You see she had lost her mother as a child, and even though at that time I could not comprehend what she said, I knew she was a wise loving woman who was sending me a message from God and I respected that.

It seemed like I was numb through the funeral but God got me through it. It felt like my heart had been ripped out. Relatives were telling me how I should be, but it was like my life was a movie, that I was watching and I was locked within myself. I remember my mom telling me to take care of the kids and I would see her face in them. My oldest son even claimed he saw her floating around the room after the funeral (She probably was).

I dreamed of her and my grandmother often and looked forward to the dreams. I cried so much and stayed to myself. One day my oldest son said mom, grandma died but we're still here. So I snapped back somehow. Every day I grew stronger. I focused on being the best mom, wife and person I could be. I struggled with the pain, but God never left me. It is weird but every time I needed her He would send me someone to comfort me.

I also learned how to comfort others. I still miss her and probably always will but I was blessed to have her in my life and I carry her love and memories in my heart. Sometimes I wish she could just be a voice in my ear like a Bluetooth wireless ear adapter and I could talk to her all the time. But you know I think God wanted me to grow and trust in His love and I have.

Life is about touching people's lives and making a difference. Loving, forgiving them and living each day as if it were your last. Death is like going into a hot furnace and emerging bronze.

When my aunt Edith died it brought back memories of my mom because she reminded me so much of her and I loved her so much also. My mom named me after her. She taught me so much about life and family and God, and I truly miss her. But I understand so much more in 2007 than I did in 1988. Jesus conquered death and that is our blessing!!----

Your cousin,

LaTresa Franchon McElrath Gray

Death Of My Dad

My Mother died when I was two. My Father married less than two months later. They were together for eight years and he married again about two months later. Two months was his magic number.

This wife was gone after two years and two months after that he went back to the last one. This time, it only lasted for two years.

In between these marriages, I had an Aunt I always went to live with until the next two months and next Mom came along. This time I had had enough. I went back to wife number two and four. She was the closest thing I could remember as a mother.

Dad moved to New Jersey and I followed a year later. A year after that, he was headed to wife number five. The only time my father hit me was the day he told me he was getting married again. I told him, "I'll be glad when you get your seven, maybe you'll stop then." That lasted three months and I headed to New York. So Dad shacked up for the next eighteen years with an older woman.

All of this leads up to one day I heard my Step Uncle say that he didn't believe my Dad loved his sister. "He just wanted a Mama for his kid." Light bulb! It was all suddenly clear. He would always say, I was his heart but I never believed him.

I thought the women were more important. It took someone else saying something bad about him for me to truly understand his love.

Here was a twenty two year old man with a two year old kid and a girl at that. All this time I was thinking "Papa Was a Rolling Stone" and he was, but he loved me too much to let my Grandparents have me. He died four years ago and I'm just grateful that I was able to find this out before he died.

Millie Jackson

Death affects individuals in many different ways. In some cultures it's looked upon as a right of passage to a better life. In others it is considerate a sacrifice.

Throughout Western culture religion is divided on this issue. Old Testament bible teaches death is considered an eye for eye. It is a form of a punishment. However, New Testament bible teachings look upon death as salvation, the rapture, the resurrection of Jesus Christ. You will be forgiven for your sins.

The interpretation of death is a consistent debate among religious scholars. I believe it is the eyes of the beholder. The expression you are born to die. I believe it is the beginning of your earthly journey. Fame Radio Disc Jockey Lynn Tolliver, signed off daily by saying "We are born to live and then we die. The middle part is up to you. Make sure you do your best.

This is safe to say in the case in the death of a parent. In the majority of cases, your parent or parents are going to give you their best. They give the precious gift of life. In addition, they are your first contact with life. Therefore you become naturally attached to them. When a parent dies it seems a part of you has died. However, it is a new beginning in your life.

A seed has been planted in you. It is an uncomfortable feeling at first. The parent has passed their legacy and their sprit onto you.

I lost my father in 1999. It has been an enlightening experience. I reflect on his sprit everyday. As a result, I became more spiritually mature. I am able to unleash strongholds that have control me, over the years. I believe death is a right of passage. It can be expected like the death of my father.

Death can be unexpected in the case of my friend Gerald Levert. Nevertheless - death is something we cannot avoid; it is up to you to make the best out of the middle.

God Bless!

Joe Stills

Five people I loved and cared about have died since November of last year. Death, killed, died, dying, passing away, making their transition, going home, going to a better place, went to live with God ,etc. Those are many of the words, phrases and/or statements people use to describe the end of a life here on earth. All of those statements have caused many, many questions for me. But the sum of all of the questions is WHY???

I understand that God is the creator and has the power to give life and take it away. What I don't get is why our creator didn't create us in a world that would not allow any illness, injustice, and overall unhappiness. I understand the free will thing that we were all given....but since God created EVERYTHING...why couldn't he see that some of his creations (people) couldn't handle it. My questions along these lines have been there since I was a child.

I have enormous faith in God to soothe all wounds and to bestow his Divine Order on all things. However, five people in five months is a bit much.

My 33 year old friend Monique (wife & mother of a two year old & a four year old) passed away from a rare genetic heart condition. My heart goes out to her parents, husband, and children, entire circle of friends and family who had so many other plans of living a life with her. We buried Monique on a beautiful day...a day just as beautiful as she was.

My cell phone rang three times as I was driving out of the cemetery. It is my sister/friend Adrienne calling to tell me that Gerald Levert is gone. Gerald and I were not close friends, but we were really cool & grew up together.

mjm barrett

161

He and I didn't speak very often because of his demanding and successful career. We were high school friends....and remained friends in spite of the huge gaps in the times we saw each other or talked. His cause of death was accidental. Once again I was overwhelmed with sadness & grief. I spent endless hours wondering how to deal with my own feelings & empathizing with his close knit family and many, many close friends.

There was nothing for me to do but add them to the long list of people I was praying for with Monique's passing. It was all too much. On January 12th I received a call from a cousin in Cleveland I never hear from. He is calling to tell me that his Mother, my favorite paternal Aunt Doris Saddler is gone. She had been ill, so it wasn't a surprise. It was actually a relief since dying was all she ever wanted to talk about.

I was happy for her to have peace and to be out of pain. Her illnesses held her hostage in her home, and her quality of life had totally diminished. As true as this was, watching my Uncle grieve adjust to the loss of his soul mate of 56 years was extremely difficult. I felt helpless because I was. There was nothing any of us could do or say to ease the pain they were experiencing.

My Uncle and Cousin were then added to the list of those I was praying for. A few months later, one of my neighbors was killed. Her name was Angel. She was five years old and was KILLED AT SCHOOL when a flagpole fell on her. How the hell does a flagpole fall on a five year old? School is supposed to be a safe place. WHY???? She and my youngest (Joshua) were a born a month apart.

mjm barrett

162

She and her brother played with my children almost every day. She was beautiful....spirited.....and fearless. She didn't share my DNA...but she was one of my children. I couldn't sleep for a week after her accident. Sleep couldn't come to me because a weird combination of sadness & despair were sharing space in my brain along with gratitude and happiness that *my* children were home with me...safe and sound...in their beds. I am totally overwhelmed by the short time we all had with her.

There were 12 other children playing near Angel when the flagpole fell. Why did they need that experience???? Her funeral was last Tuesday. But the day before her funeral, one of my best friends father was killed in a car accident. Mr. John Kendall must have had a heart attack while driving home from a golf trip. He crossed a median and hit a semi head on.

So here I am. Trying not to come a part at the seams. In a span of one week, we are dealing with the death of a five year old & a 77 year old along with the spirits of three others who have recently gone home. It's kind of ironic....the young & the old. Death does NOT discriminate. Your time is your time....whether you choose to get the most of it or not.

Angel got the most of hers for sure. It seems to me that she was here just long enough to enjoy the sunshine and wind blowing in her hair....charming all of the grown ups around her in order to buy ice cream from the ice cream truck at least once a day. She knew she was loved....and loved us all back, but she left us before her innocence and zest for life could get snuffed out by the world and all of its dysfunction.

mjm barrett

While Angel made the most of her five years on earth, the other four were blessed with many, many more. I continue to share the sadness & carry thoughts and prayers for everyone touched by the "transition" made by Monique, Gerald, Aunty Doris, Angel, and Mr. Kendall.

I am also ever so deeply grateful for those of us who are still here. My prayer for myself is that I never forget the layers of feeling I have right now. Those feelings are motivating me to slow down and spend more quality time with my children, my husband, and circle of friends.

I am also an even more patient & kind to everyone I come in contact with. They, too could be gone tomorrow. *"Slow down and enjoy"*............ *"Slow down and enjoy"*........."is what is being whispered in my ears now. "Slow down & enjoy" is what I hear when I get distracted by or stressed about "stuff". My questions are still there....but the answers really aren't required for me to go on.

Right now I know that each one of their lives has truly touched mine in a profound way. I will not ever be the same...never, ever, ever, ever.

Michelle Barrett

Death to me is extremely dark. It is the fear of the unknown. So many times many of us pretend not to be afraid, but it, no doubt, consumes so many of us with fear.

5 years ago my 50 year old Uncle, who was living with my family, had a heart attack in my 5 year old daughter's room. She found him "asleep" as she describes it and even told my husband that "Uncle Rudy is frozen". We all rushed to see him and he indeed was dead. The unfortunate part was just as I came in the door the night before I heard him walking around. I thought he was fine. It sounded as though he was having an argument with a lady friend. I heard a loud growl and now looking back I realize that he had his heart attack while I sat below on the first floor of my home.

I cry so many days wondering if I could have, if I would have, if I should have. I ponder over the fact that maybe I could have saved him. But could I have really done so? God works in mysterious ways; we never know what the ultimate plan is. We surely have to walk by faith and live by faith. As for my daughter who is now 11, the experience opened her mind to understand at a very young age that death is inevitable. As for me the fear of the unknown is no doubt still alive but the fear of losing a love one is dead. One day we will all leave this earth and hopefully we will all have left our mark.

Kym Sellers

From
John Chaffee
Inspired by his sister, Lyn Chaffee

Someone is missing at Christmas
Someone I've loved all my life
Someone I played with and laughed all night long
Someone I think of when I hear that song

Someone is missing at Christmas
Someone has left me alone
Someone so close even though we're apart
Someone who'd finish a sentence I'd start

Someone whose love is my favorite gift
Someone whose presence is my Christmas wish
Someone who always was here
Someone is missing this year

Candlelit snapshots of Christmas gone by
You in your favorite chair
Memories, like snowflakes, melt in my eyes
I look and you're not sitting there

Someone whose love is my favorite gift
Someone whose presence is my Christmas wish

Someone is missing at Christmas
Wait
Someone is touching my heart
Someone has heard me and answered my call
Someone I love is not missing at all

Someone is with me at Christmas
Someone's right here in my heart
Someone I love is with me this Christmas
And will be each Christmas to come

I read your book and I personally want to tell you that you have lifted my spirits. I lost my mother on August 1, 2006. This is my first Mother's Day without her. I have nothing but beautiful memories of her. I was in Detroit the day before she died and heard my calling to go see her. I am so glad that I am a good listener because I got to see her and kiss her one last time. I can remember her looking at me and telling me how pretty I looked. She kept staring at her baby girl.

As I was heading home I started to cry because I knew in my heart I would not see her again. The day she died I spoke to her on the phone three times that day and later that night she was gone. I come from a family of 14 and none of them heard the calling. I was my mother's pride and joy and she always called me and Billy her babies. I dream of her often and in every dream that I had since her passing I hear her say the same words. "Don't worry baby, it's all right".

I told my siblings it's what you do in a person's life not what you do in their death. My family did more in her death than in her life. I have always been there for her. I am filled with inner peace. So as I go through this first Mother's Day without her I feel as though she is right here with me. I can feel her love and warmth. Lynn this book is a God send for me. Thank you so much. Mother's Day will be much easier now.

Valerie Sparks

Death slid quietly into my life the first time when I was eight years old. Unbelievably to many my first real death experience, outside of the untimely demise of the family dog, was the death of President Kennedy.

I remember the whole emotional scene as if it were yesterday, because seeing my second grade teacher cry scared me and matured me. I realized at that moment that everybody could be reduced to human emotions regardless of how stern, educated or strict.

I listened to her speak to us between sobs and I just remember how sad I got. I didn't cry, but a segment of my child innocence was shattered. I felt like I could not afford to be a child in a world that would kill a smiling, waving father of two, President who talked as if he was going to change the plight of black people.

There was nothing that he could have done to deserve to be gunned down in the street like a bad guy from an old B western.

What I later realized when my precious grandmother succumbed to cancer was that God was preparing me for the loss of my grandmother and many other relatives over the years. I mourned for each of my relatives, and shed many tears but I never again faced death with that second grade innocence I did back in 1963.

Blanche G.

Marshall and his Godmother

Everyone has something in their life they have to live with. My mother passed away and my wife passed away one year later. It was hard for me, but God picked me up and let me know I had to go on and I did. I am thankful for his blessing.

Marshall Thompson
Leader of the Chi-Lites

Happiness

this dying thing...

HAPPINESS

Happiness is not whether you are rich or poor.
     There are poor people who are extremely happy, and there are rich people who are terribly sad. So money does not determine your status of enjoyment. This does not mean, do not try to make all the money you can for your financial security. Some rich people don't want poor people to have anything. I'm not saying don't try – I'm just saying – money will not make you happy. It may bring you relief… Forget the saying; – money is *not* the root of all evil. There are people who do evil things for free. Understand what evil is – and do whatever you can to keep it from your life.
Happiness is not whether you are fat or skinny.
     I've seen some of the happiest, jolly heavy set people. And I've seen skinny people who were miserable in life. Just plain bitter. It isn't weight to determine your contentment in life. Should you be at a healthy weight for a better quality of life? Probably, but, if you are heavyweight, you can still have a smile on your face and a happy heart.
Happiness is not determined by your race.
     Asians are happy, and there are unhappy Asians. There are happy Africans and unhappy Africans. There are happy Jews and unhappy Jews. No race holds the key to extreme and complete bliss, and on the other hand, no race holds the key to the bitter end. Everyone can feel the heat of the sunshine at one point. Only a geographical position will prevent that. Fear exposes itself to all. If you want to be happy, you can be.

remember the times we shared a
love, back when all we had...

was each other?

Happiness is not where you live.

Men exist who have the 'prettiest' wife, and live in a _luxurious home_ and sad. There are women who have EVERYTHING. _Live in the right neighborhood_, have the guy they dreamed of, but are miserable for some reason. There are some who _live with their parents_ and are beside themselves with joy, and some who live with their parents and think they are enduring hell. Happy gets its true thrust from within. Happy is a choice you make, in spite of the odds against you.

Happiness is not what you do.

You could be a teacher, and happy at it, or it could be the most miserable thing, or you could be disenchanted because of something else. Teaching could be your means of support, while you are happy because you have the man or woman you want. There are happy dentists, and unhappy dentists.

A person could be doing construction, or an architect. Your profession could be a farmer, or a singer. I've seen unhappy singers, and I've see happy farmers. Your job will not determine whether or not you're happy. You will, and you can.

Don't get me wrong, you could be miserable, and because you have a lovely home, that makes you happy. You could have a terrible home and you can't wait to get to work and be happy. But it's for sure, if you set your goals for the unobtainable, you will fail. Be realistic – Try to live a practical life, and find things that make you happy. Life is a precious commodity. Your trip to the end can be a pleasant journey, or it could be the worse ride you'll ever have. The choice is yours.

Happiness **IS**, what you are inside and how you feel about yourself – Happiness is a state of mind. Don't you want to be happy? Or at least as happy as you can be?

Live the absolute, find reality.

Happiness awaits each and every one of you!

this Dying thing

When Life Stops

I remember when I was younger, but not too young, perhaps in my mid-to-late thirties, I would see older people just break into a cry. And at my age, I haven't got into that yet, but I was reading one of the other contributing writers, which happens to be my cousin Verdelle's portion, I couldn't stop crying. To tell you the truth, I couldn't finish reading it, my emotion became overwhelming and I had to stop.

The 50s, 60s, 70s, and 80s to give you a safe margin, didn't feature too many crying men. Even though men have tear ducts in their optical system, you were supposed to suck it in. Hold that grief, so when people see you, they only witness your manhood, not your feminine side.

Because a man cooks, is he less of a man? Should women not want to play basketball? And so a man sews, isn't being a tailor a credible profession? Thus the tear theory. We have had our growth stifled due to old rules and regulations that were not true and never will be true.

I cried at my sister's funeral, I cried at my mother's funeral. I watch movies where a mother is dying, or someone, and I immediately get hit in the emotional pocket, and water pours down my face. And I don't care what you think of that, or what you think of me. If people have been in your life, like my family has been in mine, tears have to be a release, like a safety valve or a fuse, so you don't blow your lid. I think tears are a pressure trigger, a stress outlet.

None of us invented the body, a marvelous machine of life, and tears were a part of your existence since the day you were born. And not all babies cry when they come out of the womb, but I would venture to say, most of them do. (They probably want to go back in). I think all of our body parts have a purpose, and tears are probably overlooked as a vital part of our existence. More than likely, ten, fifteen years from now, they will probably discover, we'll live a lot longer, if we would have cried and displayed our sorrow, than had we kept it in. All this medicine we are taking, and we have all the remedies and medicines within ourselves.

Letting you know, I don't have any answers as to what is the right thing to do, or the wrong thing. Psychologists probably have the right answer, but opt to keep you coming back every week in half-hour or hour increments, so they can continue to make unlimited revenue gains. That's the way of the world, it seems. Consultants, don't tell you how to fix anything without a contract for a year, or a term that suffices them. Why isn't there anyone that tells you something in a lump and move on to the next trouble? No one would make any money if they operated that way.

When life stops, it begins a profit machine for millions, everywhere. Why mess up a good thing, just to get people focused in the right direction? If someone can't money off the misery and pain of others – what good is this whole life thing? As I stated in my book, ROUGH wRITERS, in the "Who Can You Trust Section", the real actors are the people you see everyday. When life stops, and it can be very dramatic for many whom charade and masquerade, because we really can't deal with it..

We are openly, subliminally desensitized to the stopping of life. When John Wayne died in one film – he was 'alive' again in his next spectacular footage of movie. If you see Samuel L. Jackson get hurt, near death in one scene – the next scene he's all healed, and practically clean, it's like watching Daffy Duck get his beak shot off by Elmer Fudd, and in the very next frame, Daffy's got a new face, all shiny and bright.

How many times has the bad guy in a cowboy western, get beat to death, and come back again and again as the bad guy, and die once more? What kind of implication has been visually hidden without wolf-in-sheep's clothing set in our mind, about death? It is for sure, if the good portions of a movie leave an impression, like in Play It Forward, there are some of us out there who see a character die repetitively, then sprout up again in another hit flick. Haven't you said, probably, and don't remember thinking or saying to someone, "I thought he was dead"

nature's mist of life

When life stops on TV, it keeps going. When life stops at the theatre, it keeps going. When life stops in real life – it stops. I'm sure there are death scenes in plays, where the actors and actresses are live on stage, and when the skit is finished, all of the actors come out and take a bow, even the one or ones that died in the display. Wouldn't it be better if the ones who died in the play, not come out and take a bow, so we can see what it's like when life stops, really? Oh yeah, I forgot, they'll be back tomorrow night to do it again, so it doesn't really matter.

Regardless of the device we spectacle for what we are entertained by, when death is portrayed, it puts everything on hold for a moment or two, then onward.

When life stops for a father, then later for another family member, do they connect somewhere out there? Do we meet again? Does life stop here on earth and continue somewhere else? If you had 'choice' friends and family, are we all in the same neighborhood, or within flying distance? Or is it, you only get to pick ten of your best connects, like a mobile phone deal?

If a woman married four times, and all of her husbands died before her, when she dies, is she in the vicinity with all of them, similar to a commune, or the Smurfs? There was only one girl in that cartoon the Smurfs, and I'm just being silly, to break up any sorrow, because death is full of sorrow. And I must say, right about now, I think I'm happy that I can still joke around, and still laugh after those three major players of mine are no longer here. That's them in me, and I appreciate whatever they said, or whatever did, to get me here, left behind without them. When Life Stops – it can be the saddest thing you EVER experience. When Life Stops in the news, we watch it, as an information source, and as entertainment. I've heard critics say that all the violence we see on television whatever the topic is about, the killings – lessens the blow of how severe dying is. And that is not the exact words, but close to the point of it. I'm going to disagree with that, because if that was valid – very few people would cry now, and if any of you witnessed WHEN THE LEVEES BROKE, or NINE ONE ONE – you saw a lot of sentiment and tears. A LOT.

By now with all the slaughters and murders we have witnessed, we would be all cried out, and we're not. We waste a lot of time saying things that do nothing for our growth. We go along with tons of items in our faces that have little if any value for becoming better human beings. When Life Stops, the games begin. Now is the time to ask father for that money, because he is sad that momma is gone, and that stern strong exterior he use to have has been chiseled down to a mere windbreaker unable to stop a storm, what he really needs is a cement shelter, and he can be reached now.

Now is the time to steal merchandise from an employer who has been exceptionally good to us, because she just lost her parents in a plane crash, and she has her back turned on her business. When life stops – a whole new wave of things will come at you and my final thoughts here – At a time when the church can really be beneficial to you, and you have to answer this on your own, it's my question, but it's your answer – does the guy in charge whether he's a minister, or reverend, a pastor or pope, a rabbi or deacon, (and it could be a she), does that person say things to make you feel better and move on, or do they tell you things that you think sound good, but only make you feel worse, for their benefit? Was there a trick delivery?

When life stops.

This Dying Thing

Funerals

Funerals

Right off the bat, I'm going to tell you, I don't like funerals. I can count on both hands of the funerals, or visiting of the dead at a funeral home. I don't think I'll attend too many more, that would depend upon who it was for me, not for you. I told my niece, and it may be written in another area here, I will be the only one at my mother's funeral for me. I said that to Michelle Tolliver, too, David's wife. It wasn't meant to be malicious or hateful – I'm not into that. I have been, and probably still do exist in a revengeful state at times, but I have never been hateful, ... in my life.

Revenge takes a lot of energy, to think about, to plot or plan, and for the common person, the one that just wants to have it as easy as possible through this journey, takes a lot of time, it's just too much. HATE probably takes ten times those elements I mentioned before, unless you are working with evil, then it comes natural.

Funerals, to me are sad. No matter how many times the speaker or God connection tells you it's a time to rejoice, we don't. I will tell you, when I was the master of ceremonies for the Gerald Levert "celebration of life", there were a lot of moments of laughter and joy, but there were many tears. It got to me when I hugged Eddie Levert, Sr, Gerald's father.

There is the atmosphere of folks who come, just to be seen. They do not care about the dead, they do not care about the pain inside that house, they just do not care. I think you should install a security device that detects guns or objects of destruction, but it would be an emotion device that detects the frauds that want to pass into the funeral proceeding and it goes off when a fake walks through those bars. That would be good for a lot of things, love relationships, friends – an alarm would trigger if the person coming to this event wasn't true. Wouldn't that save a lot of time and energy? Don't expect to see that any time too soon.

Right off the bat, I'm going to tell you – I'm a little uneasy about funerals. It can be a cleansing of one's soul here. Some of the stronger people that you have witnessed have been brought to their knees, for the thoughts they are thinking.

If you have regrets, it may come out – you didn't get a chance to do what you wanted to do, to say what you wanted to say, to ask forgiveness. Fortunately for my sanity, I do not have any regrets. It's the final time you will see them in human form, if you are lucky enough not to have lost them viciously, or reconstructively. None of my major three had a closed casket. That has got to be a hell no one wants to visit either.

And probably the tone of the people who perform the ceremony. They seem to act more dead than the main character(s). I'm sure by now, if they have been in business for a few months, what attachment could they have? They should be yucking it up, because it is going to cost us to bury someone. They should at least smile, and maybe that's the problem for me. Maybe I think they are being phony about this whole ordeal. They bury people everyday. They should be use to this; maybe it would make people feel better about their dearly departed – maybe not.

Maybe they did laugh in the beginning, and were told, this is not the time. But like us. There are many news stories about people, who died in Idaho, and you live in Montana – you didn't know them, should it be terrible for you? Death is a daily occurrence.

I will honestly tell you, hearing other people cry did not make me cry. When I saw Kevin Chillious at the funeral, because we grew up together, it was when my mother was alive. When I saw Antonio Marshall – a relatively newcomer, he was there, because my mother died. My good friend Tom Kent and his wife Karen. They made the special trip to the funeral, because my mother died. I saw Morris Edwards. His mother and MY mother were very close friends. I sang in the Glee Club at church with Morris Edwards and Mrs. Jessie Edwards, his mother who was the director.

My cousins came from Detroit, Michigan. Avis, Pudgy, that crew, it reminded me when my father died – when my sister died, and now they are here for my MOTHER. That's what made me cry.

There were quite a few people who came to Momma T's funeral. Forgive me if I didn't mention your name, but believe me, whatever you thought of my family to attend – God bless you.

And I don't think it's because the funeral makes you cry, I'm crying now – I will cry forever until the day I die, inside and outside, it should be a known fact, the crying from me, doesn't bother me, if you see me cry. I probably don't like funerals because I know they mean for me, because I'm at it – it was someone that held a special place in my mere existence that was vitally, vitally important.

I had my father for 27 years. I had my sister for 38 years. I had my mother for 56 years, almost 57 – that's what makes me cry and the funeral just puts it all on point.

I will say this again, because it is the truth for me. I would rather have the pain of their death in my mind while I'm alive, than to have the pain of their absence as a reason or purpose they existed. Can you imagine all the people that have parents and siblings and they mean nothing to them? That *does* exist, and I wouldn't want to think about a funeral like that, where the person didn't count in your life. A quick question – to you. Do you count in somebody's life? Does it matter? Will you ever find a question to that, or you too hung up on you – I'm not judging you, I'm just asking you. You don't have to find me, to tell me, you might even want to throw this book away – and that would be okay with me, too.

I will tell you right off the bat, I don't like funerals. Didn't like the first one, probably won't like any of them, but maybe mine, who knows?

A **funeral** closes the chapter on that relationship in the worldly meaning, and maybe that's why I don't like funerals.

185

This DYING THING

Suicide

Suicide

All the other ways of death are not by the choice of the person in question. If you are murdered, it's not your decision. If it's an accident, you didn't vote for or against it. And from natural causes which include illness – not your nod.

I have never been at a point in my life, where I wanted to pull the plug on me. When I was younger, I tried to hold my breath as long as I could and see what would happen, but the body's self preservational desire for air, burst my mouth open, and I was breathing again. And let's note that presevational is not a word recognized by the word program's spell check, but a word I wanted to use, because it sounded good. *You figure out the meaning.* And forgive me if you think I'm making a joke about this section, I am *not*. I knew someone who tried to commit suicide, and I will refrain from the name because I don't want repercussion from it spreading in thought because someone you know now has made that attempt, and you're related to them.

Suicide is probably the only death that we question, if it comes to finding out a reason why. If you say a person was shot, or stabbed or beat, you know they were one of those. If the person had cancer, or pneumonia, maybe an aids complication – there's your answer. If they got hit by a car, or an object fell from a higher floor on them, sad as you may be, you've got the answer, but if a person takes their own life – you want to know why. What were they thinking about, what were they going through? Maybe if I could have talked to them, or if someone was able to talk to them, it could have been prevented.

Another reason they say suicide is committed is to get back at someone. To prove a point. There have been individuals who have set themselves on fire, for the world to see. They are making a statement. They generally leave a note. I know you have seen movies where someone is killed and the party involved, tries to make it 'look' like a suicide. What a world, huh?

Matlock, Monk, Psych, Law & Order, CSI and many other broadcasts entertainment productions all have had segments where there was an apparent suicide, and everybody else was ready to wrap it up, but the star of the show proves otherwise, it was not a suicide, it was murder. Is it possible that the way we see suicide on TV, makes us assume this is the way suicide is for everyone? Was the person who committed suicide, "*a certain way*"? Was that person a suicide contestant, meaning a candidate for self destruction? Do you see anyone in your life, whether it be a neighbor, friend, or relative? And what makes you think that about them? I think if sorrow and sadness was the element that turns you, half of the world would be gone, and further, I don't think we'll ever get there, our focus is not on life -

I worked with a woman that had a husband who committed suicide. Probably my first, close affiliation with that. If you go back and read the death of a love relationship, it can clue you. With what the woman was doing, and this is just my guess, she was probably driving this guy nuts. Thank the Lord; I have not been in a relationship like that. And you never know, many of us may only be seconds or inches away from something like that. Here's another reason to count your blessings if you're not. And that is a tough statement, because if you're fed up with whatever, your health, a situation, an unpleasant discovery about you, you may opt out. It's that mind thing again, which we will probably never ever get to the bottom of. He was probably aware of what was going on, and couldn't deal with it – I don't know, this is my speculation.

Phyllis Hyman took her life. There were rumors that she was unhappy with her career. She had several songs that appeared to be career accomplishments. I think I met her once in the 70s, she was less than a year older than I was, and all the men would swoon over her. One of her songs, "Old Friend" was a gay woman anthem.

Let your eyes behold, the beauty that nature has to offer…..

She had sex appeal, she was touring – and if I have my information correct, she was on tour when she ended it all. And I thought to myself – she had men after her, (maybe not the right one). She was working and had quite a few albums that garnered a lot of attention and radio exposure. You can't tell what is on the inside, by looking at the outside. She was beautiful.

But did 'she' think she was beautiful? You would be surprised at your attraction to someone who has a grip on the way you think, they tell you something and it becomes what you think forever, even to your detriment. I can't tell you what made her do it, but I use to have almost a life-sized poster of her for years. Now that I think of it, I still can't believe she took the suicide route. I thought everything was going her way.

I use to play INXS's "What You Need" all the time, because it was a very powerful up-tempo song, and remembrance of the days when I worked at WGCL-FM, Cleveland, now WNCX. The video of that song was electrifying. They featured a lot of freeze frame action that you cannot duplicate live on stage unless you have a screen on stage, people can stop, but they can't do it like it's done in video production. Michael Jackson's "Billy Jean" is the same way. The news came on, Michael Hutchence, member of INXS committed suicide. I didn't get it – but of course we'll never get it. A big rock star, must have it all. You see, material things are not everyone's goal in life. Unless you're inside that person's brain to see what they see – you may never know, because some don't want to tell you what they are thinking, they will tell you what they think you want to hear. I later discovered that he use to date Kylie Minogue, who sang one of my younger sons' favorite songs, "Can't Get You Out Of My Head". After marveling the video on that, because of Kylie – I thought to myself, maybe it was because of her. She had to be, but you never know.

There is an abundance of suicides. Probably more than we would like to know about, when it relates to us personally. And are suicides troubling to us, because we really care about the people who took the out option, or is it just our curiosity of why that person did it, or what were they going through? Can suicide be passed down, like other hereditary tags?

I wrote a song called **The Suicide Song**.

I'm gonna take my life, with my own hands.
I'm gonna take my life, with my own hands.
I don't understand why I have sorrow.
I won't have to worry about tomorrow.
I've got pain
And all my problems remain.

I'm gonna take my life and throw it away.
I'm gonna take my life and throw it away.
I don't have to think about what you say.
I won't have to worry about today.
I've got pain
And all my problems remain.

I wrote that when I was about 17, so it was based on what I thought about suicide at that time. I didn't have any clinical data, nor did I do any research. I just picked a subject, threw those words together and there you are. And here we are, still no closer to anything, or do I think we will ever be.

THIS DYING THING

REMEMBER REMEMBER REMEMBER

REMEMBER

song by David Payton / Pat Frances

Remember - The games we use to play –
Remember - The words we use to say –

When I said that I loved you, and you said you loved me too

Remember - The Sun would always shine –
Remember - I was yours, and you were mine –
Remember - Yes I knew it in my heart
Remember - It was true love at the start

You took sick one day, I saw it in your eyes
You never told me, but I knew and how I cried
When the doctor said, you didn't have much time
That you would die soon, I went out of my mind
You left the next day, just at the crack of dawn
You never know how much you love one, not until they're gone
I was lonely; there was nothing I could do
Kept hear you saying "Remember, I'll always love you!"

Remember - The games we use to play –
Remember - The words we use to say –

When I said that I loved you, and you said you loved me too

Remember - The Sun would always shine –
Remember - I was yours, and you were mine –
Remember - I am lonely, and I'm blue
Remember - You said, "I'll always love you!"

REMEMBER

This portion of the book is about people that I have known to the best of my knowledge and the death of that person. There have been quite a few people that have died in my life. The ones that have been the closest to me, have had an everlasting effect, but if you were raised like I was – you keep going. I don't think it's effective to stop because someone else has stopped living.

Evidence, because of the growth of the population of the world tells you that most people move forward. Through the tragedies that life has, the perils, so-to-speak, if you check the world population in 1900, and check it in 1950, and currently, you will see steady growth – through all the disasters that nature throws us, and all of the devastation we bring on ourselves.

There are storms that take lives, and volcano eruptions. And mudslides – you name it – tsunami and earthquakes. Mass murderers and war. Let's not leave war out, because war takes a lot of people and the world is still left with the same problem.

The ability to keep your head above water and your thoughts positive; to keep living. I think if we were raised to stop when death hits us, there would be few people. There are some who take death serious and others who look at it lightly. It is for sure, it is something we will all face, with those around us, and then eventually we will hit it directly, head on.

You've read where other people contributed their stories, and now the people that I know. You may read about someone who reminds you about someone, or just the fact that you witness pain and sorrow as we all do, maybe that will make you feel better about it. And this. I know a lot of people who should have died other than those who did, but as you look around you – death doesn't work like that. Like a fair death. I know you would like to have some people here on earth forever with you, but death doesn't work like that. And on a positive note – neither does LIFE.

David Payton

david
(of men at large, when he was little),
my sister, Donita,
my father, then my mother -
in my father's lap, was Verdelle
and me on the corner,
beneath David.

UNCLE VICK

I may have this wrong, but I think this was the first death that I remember that had meaning for someone close to me. His name was Uncle Vick, his last name was Jackson. He wasn't a blood relative to the Nix side of the family, but he was married to one of my favorite people – Auntie. I didn't know until much later her first name was Esther. Everybody called her Auntie. Uncle Vick was her husband.

He had a name for my sister and me. He called us Duke & Bodo. I don't know whether or not he liked kids or anything. He didn't appear to be a mean man, I think he played with us a little, but not like a parent, not like an uncle. I don't know whether he had children or not, but he and Auntie didn't have children together. He also called my cousins, Lesita and Latresa, Catch 'em and Smell 'em. There you go – what does *that* mean? Duke and Bodo, and which was Duke, me? Or was I Bodo? Catch 'em and Smell 'em. To me, now that I look back, he probably didn't like kids, but you never know. I think derivatives from your original name would have had more significance, although I have called a couple of kids a name that didn't mean anything in reference to their name, but I love *my* kids, and kids that have been in my life for one reason or another.

He had to take a pill that he had to put under his tongue, and he couldn't have a lot of salt in his diet. But I wasn't really thinking about it, to me, he wasn't the main player, it was Auntie. And I had no idea I would be writing about him now, in 2007, because my mother died, so I don't have any accurate records on most of these deaths.

We arrived at Auntie's house and the paramedics were taking him out. I think they may have tried to revive him or something, but he never came back. That particular death didn't affect me at all. And it didn't look like it had an effect on my Auntie either, because we kept going over there every Sunday after church. We went over Auntie's house when he was alive and we went there after he died. With or without him. Maybe that is where I got the saying, "Life goes on - with or without you."

One of the symbols for our
dearly departed. A cross,
with an arrangement of
flowers at the bottom. Do
we do this for them, or do
we do this for us?

COMER PAYTON NIX SR.

The most I remember about my grandfather on my mother's side, or maternal as you would categorize it, was many of the things my mother would tell me.

Let me tell you how connected I was with my mother, so you'll understand. And I'm not saying I am any different than anyone regarding a relationship with their parents, but I remember as a little boy, if my mother *pretended* to cry, I would cry. I couldn't have been older than six or seven. I remember her doing that once and I will probably elaborate on this later when I write about her, but I really, really loved my mother.

You probably don't know this about yourself, or maybe you do, but have you ever seen a child that wanted to do something regardless of what you wanted, and if that child got hurt, they still wanted to do as they wished? Then something else happens, that was not as painful, honestly, and they acted like someone was hanging them?

We learn at an early age how to manipulate. If you are fortunate enough to have two great parents, one will say, "he's okay, let him play", probably the father, and the mother will probably try to cradle you. We do things on some occasions, based on the response we get. We avoid things or act a certain way, depending upon what reaction we see, from the people we love and love us.

That was the way it was for me. The man who instilled discipline in his children, a carry through for what little discipline I probably have inside this gut of mine, was my mother's father. I'm sure she loved him dearly, as her other eight brothers and sisters is why it moved her and why it had an effect on me.

It meant something to her. I probably watched things, even before my father got me to the next level of my being observant. It didn't stop her – a lot of my learning from her came from how I saw her, and this put skids on her speed, but it did not bring her to a halt, she kept going. It looked like he raised his kids like soldiers. The girls in the family wore hi-top shoes, which meant their ankles were covered. To me their dresses looked like gowns, so they were well below their knees. If you were attracted to the Nix girls, it was their face or their minds. I don't think their bodies were out there. That came from my grandfather. He was a mailman and a mason. He had two jobs, I don't know what the other job was, but he was a hard working man.

All of his children were hard workers, and on a positive course in life. I think his way of life was so strong, that if any of them fell into a ditch, it wouldn't have taken too much for them to dig themselves out. That's a powerful parent, and with little to work with back then. But he was that good. I don't think I could have been happy if he was MY father, but he was hers and their father. I saw them take a dip, but they all progressed, like ants on a mission, even if some prank playing kid set them on fire or sprays them with Raid. They get right back into the swing of things, like the Nix family did. It was probably the way he raised them to.

She got back on the tracks of LIFE, and moved forward, so I marked that in my memory of the dearly departed. This was the second death I remember. It wasn't a powerful jab, but a little bit more meaningful, than the previous.

ESTHER JACKSON

My Auntie was the first person who died in my life that made me stand up and take a serious look at death. This was well before 1977, before my father died. She would call me Argon. Which was her derivative of the way my parents called me Are In. And they all had the right to call me what they wanted to, but let me take this time to tell you how I think it is. My name is spelled Orrin. I am going to the store OR I am going IN the gymnasium. See? OR IN. Orrin. Anyway, she called me ARGON. Are Gun. I never corrected her. My love for her had to be through my mother's love for her.

Every Sunday, we would end up at my aunt's house. She cooked fried chicken, and it was delicious. I don't know whether or not Auntie could have children, or if she ever had any, or what, but she was always happy to see us. This was the Nix side of the family.

And if you ask me, that's how true love should be among friends and family. Things that don't have any bearing on your life personally, shouldn't really concern you. I don't ever remember asking my Auntie if she had any kids, or why she didn't have children, we just went over to her house and we were happy to be there. I don't think the absence of her husband changed the atmosphere any. It didn't get worse; it couldn't have got any better than it was. I don't ever remember being 'third degreed' or questioned about any of our activity – real love. Real family love, next to none. Yes, this is the way true relationships should be.

She would have little peppermint candies, mixed with Spanish peanuts in a little silver flip-top pan, and we could have all we wanted, with our parents' permission of course, but Auntie could override their decision if our parents said no. My sister and I were brought up, not to ask for seconds, and we NEVER did. But with Auntie, it was like an additional mother. She was never unhappy to see us, ever.

My mother told me that Auntie always listened to my radio show. She was one of the two people that taught me, do what you like to do, if you could and I assumed that would make you happy, because I never saw Auntie sad or miserable, even when Uncle Vic died. Esther Jackson, always watched or listened to the Cleveland Indians, the baseball team in Cleveland, listened to my show all the time, and loved us coming over to see her, at least every Sunday, if not sometimes during the week.

I was told that she would watch me for my mother and father when they did what they had to do, whatever that was, and I would cry my eyes out when my parents left. I don't remember that, but that is what they told me.

I was also told that the only way she could stop me from crying was, to take me down into the basement and turn all the lights off. I would immediately stop crying. That may explain why I am afraid of the dark, TO THIS DAY, but I don't have any ill feelings toward her for that. Until I was told that, I just thought I was afraid of the dark. I don't like the dark, and that could be a religious thing, you know, come out of the dark – into the light?

I also remember when I was a little boy, when I was over Auntie's house, I would sit in this hi-chair and would push my feet on her kitchen table and lean the chair back. Both her and my mother (I remember) told me to stop doing it, but I didn't, so you know what happened. I pushed the chair back over and I hit my head on the iron heater and they both rushed to my crying little self and did every thing they could to sooth my pain. It was then that I learned, you better do what your elders tell you to do, because I remember balling to no end. I don't remember getting hurt though, I was told all the time I was hard-headed, and I had a hard head, which are two different meanings, but I'm sure you understand.

I couldn't believe that she died, and I knew that more dying was coming. That was the most terrible death I had experienced, which leads me to this. A lot of us take life for granted. Too many of us do not appreciate all the good in our lives, and miss opportunities to do the many things we can do, to have a happy life.

Are there abrupt endings, where we think someone has been taken too soon? Yes, but the way some of us act, it appears that we are not taken soon enough. And by no means, am I incited to experience suicide or to commit murder. But too much of the complaining people do – if they would spend that negative time, doing something they like that they can do, or doing something constructive with a more realistic expectation, I think they can raise their happiness level.

I never saw or heard my Auntie complain. She was practical and realistic. She lived alone, but had people that lived on the second and third floor, paying her rent. A couple of them were relatives. It was a huge house. A basement, first through third floor. The third floor was actually the attic, converted into prime living quarters. That was exciting to me.

There was even a picture in a collection somewhere, of me with my favorite boy cousin, (of course he's a man now, older than me by 6 days) Freddie Harper. That house had a lot of memories, but it was all centered around Esther Jackson. She was a good wholesome person with incredible values, in my observation of her. I don't think she enjoyed the services of another man after her husband died. You never know what has happened in a person's life for the decisions that they make.

She use to burn onions on the stove, so money would come. And she was the first person who said that her hand would itch, and that meant you were going to get some money. I still think that sometimes, although I doubt if it is true. But it seemed like it worked for her. I didn't see any effect on my mother when Auntie died, but my mother was good at keeping any pain, sorrow or negativity alive. I do know that the impact of not going over her house on Sunday was a major change that we all had to adjust to.

She is the Esther of the Jimmie Esther name I use on some of my projects. God had to plant her within my existence to help balance off the bad with her goodness for my life down the stretch. She had a very vital part in the person I have become. The good parts, not the bad. You never know who is watching what you do, and how it will affect your life, and you may never ever realize who you have seen that may change who you are, or what you do.

MILLARD MICHAEL FREEMAN (MIKE LOVE)

The first time I worked with Mike Love was at a radio station in Cleveland, Ohio, WJMO. We were young. We would kid around, and being a former well-known radio announcer, I saw Mike as becoming the same. He had a lot of energy and was gaining a lot of popularity. One of the fortunate things for me, and also a disadvantage at times, was, I was extremely popular, so I didn't run into those problems that exist when the boss was not as popular as the guys he was over, I was the boss and the most popular. That took a lot of jealous and envy from the game, because I have never been jealous of what another man or woman had. It allowed better relationships. We had a lot of fun working together.

Youngstown, Ohio was the second time I had association with Mike Love – He worked at a station called WGFT. I don't know what the station is now, but I worked for MCA Records, and selected that city to take product to, to get airplay. I even suggested him using Michael "My Endless" Love. Endless Love was the record sang by Lionel Richie & Diana Ross on Motown. When you are working with people that you consider a friend, or somebody you've known for a long time, it's not really work; you look forward to doing what you have to do for a living, as opposed to dread getting up everyday to do something you don't like.

What made Youngstown something was, I don't like going over bridges. He had mentioned the Meander Lake, which you have to cross when going to Youngstown, and he had previously made trips taking the same route to Pittsburgh, in Beaver Falls. There is a bridge there, which, if you are not into heights, like we both were not – you thank God, when you get across. It is that high off the ground. I think that was the biggest thing we had in common, our fear of going over bridges. Find Kevin Chillious, a childhood friend – he sometimes asks me if I remember me telling him when we crossed that Beaver Falls bridge, to roll the windows up, and then saying, what is rolling the windows going to do?

The final time was at WZAK, at the time, the King of Cleveland radio. There was a small battle to get him to work for us, and to get him to work for the competitor at the time, which was WJMO, and we won. When you play, and it really matters, you're in a competitive work arena, *you must play to win*. We had a great staff of people who worked at the station. It was located at 1729 Superior, Suite 401.

Michael had a few problems with his health. Fortunately enough, it didn't affect his working at the station, but he had a couple of bouts with some things in relationship to his kidneys. I believe he had to go on a dialysis machine once or twice a week. I don't exactly know what that thing does, but I know there are a lot of people doing that. He always kept a bright up-tempo attitude. He was very positive, and brought the shot of adrenaline the station needed at the time.

I think it was a Sunday. He called me and said he was in the hospital; it was a serious cold or something like that. I told him, don't worry about anything. He told me, he thought he was almost out of here, but it was just some kind of virus or something, and he would probably be back at work on Tuesday. We laughed and joked over the phone, me not really knowing what it could have been, but he sounded okay.

That was the last time I talked to him. The next day he died from an aneurysm. The good thing about this was I knew he was happy that he was working at WZAK. If things sour and you're in a miserable situation, that can be sad, but he was very content in his professional life. I don't know how his on-going illness weighed on his mind, he never complained about that.

A week later, his mother died. Millard Michael Freeman was an only child, and though he didn't comment much about his personal agenda – I'm sure they were extremely close. It appeared after Mike's death, she had nothing to live for.

205

DWAYNE GREGORY

When I was 17, I had this friend, Dwayne Gregory. He was my best friend at the time; you know you go through a lot of 'best' friends. And some of us have the same best friend forever. He was slightly older than I was. We lived in a relatively new area; it was the Tarkington/Lee area, close to the Harvard/Lee area. John F. Kennedy was a new high school in that vicinity. There were a cluster of us friends, the Echols brothers, Earl & Erwin, Ricky & Greg Hood, The Benfords - Harold Martin. Randolph Bolden, the Wentz gang. The Boyds, we were a rather closely knit gang of guys, always playing street ball, had a large park a short distance away, where we could play 'tackle' football.

We were a young community, and in our elementary, junior high school, and high school years. The roads were cylinder bits, we didn't have sidewalks, and we were in Cleveland, Ohio. The bus transportation was about 2 miles from where we lived, and our mailboxes were at the end of the street.

It was a strange place for most of us, who had our mail delivered to our doors, and the bus stop was just at the corner. I know in this world today, there are people who don't have bus service, or get mail delivered near, but when you're use to it, to move to a place where you've never been exposed to those things was quite different.

To make a long story short, Dwayne and I stayed home from school one day and due to circumstances, I suggested we run away. I was only joking, but he was passionately for it. The story could be a movie, it is packed with adventure. Not knowing all of the grief a parent goes through when a child is missing, we didn't have that as obvious as it is now, with the child alert, the milk cartons, you know what exists today for missing people.

When we came back and both sets of our parents were waiting to see us, my parents were happy, not so with Dwayne. He told our little group of guys, his step-father whipped him, extremely ferociously. Those weren't his words, but hopefully, you get the depth of what I'm trying to say he said. My parents were just glad to see me back, okay. You see I didn't really have anything to run away about. It was just a joke to me. We were poor, but I wasn't really unhappy.

Dwayne and I were also in a group, with Alvin Thomas, Gerald Thomas, Alvin Hall and the two of us. The Thomas's, Halls, and Dwayne lived on 175th, very close to each other on the same side of the street, and I lived on 176th street.

He use to sing, "I've got money in my pocket". He would sing that over and over, so I added, "I've got money in my pocket and I feel blue – You know why, Cause I lost you – You've gone and left me, deserted and painful, and I feel it's so down right shameful."

He would sing the lead to that song, and we would practice. We were going to be a big group with hits one day. I don't think Alvin and his brother Gerald got along, so we drifted apart. But I was able to work with Dwayne with his step-father with his janitorial company. This is where I saw that in a short period of time, Dwayne's step-father was able to buy the equipment he needed, and pay for the station wagon he used for the cleaning service in less than a year. To me, that was incredible. Where it took 3 or 4 years to pay for a vehicle, they had it paid for in less than a year – what an inspiration to go into business for yourself.

We later got hooked up with the wrong crowd, were a guy who was much, much older than our normal crew started hanging out with us, which meant drugs for some, and fights, so this is where Dwayne and I started to drift apart.

He disappeared totally out of my life for a long period of time, but I learned he married and had children. I was out shopping one night, and saw where he was a manager at a store. We talked briefly, but we didn't change numbers or anything. He died shortly after that, which shocked me, because it didn't look like anything was wrong. He appeared to be a healthy person. Although we had some fairly close times, I don't think his death affected me, as it would have when I heard about it, if we were the friends we were when we were young. I never expected him to die as young as he did, but as my mother told me, in my theory of her teachings, do we ever expect anyone to die, even when they are dying? There are many different phases and things we go through, or nothing – death comes in many shapes or sizes, death comes in different colors. It is for sure, death comes...

man can be "one" with nature

The Gerald Levert Farewell

by Lynn Tolliver jr. (as printed in Internet Pioneer website, Urban Insite, Nov 2006)

For those of you, who really know me; know I am terribly afraid to fly. I fly for family - Gerald Levert was family. Because I'm going to try to keep this as personal-free as possible, I am going to keep the family's names out of this, but still going to tell you about the send off for one of Cleveland's finest sons of all time.

When I first connected with the family, a cousin, they asked me if I could speak at the farewell, and I told the person I was going to let him know the next day. That was my fear of flying getting in the way. I called that person back in an hour and told them, I would be there.

The flight to Cleveland from Tampa was split into two flights, so that meant I had to take off and land twice, but that was a sacrifice I was willing to make for "like a little brother to me", G Levert.

Upon arriving at the venue, which had been changed from the 3000 seat capacity, to an 11,000 seat capacity because of the many people who had lined up at Music Hall, the person in charge of the celebration handed me what I thought was going to be some basic outlines to follow in what I was going to say. It was at that point I was made aware I was going to be the Master of Ceremonies for Gerald Levert's farewell.

I was shocked, but at the same time honored, because they could have selected anyone they wanted to, and I want to let you everyone know, I was honored and humbled - I just went out and tried to do the best that I could.

If I wasn't at the event, I would have never known to what great extent Gerald had touched so many lives. I knew he was a ladies' delight, I knew there were a lot of people who really appreciated what musical contributions Gerald has made to the industry, but I had no knowledge of all the people that had from a few moments, to a few months to the many mega-periods the stroke of -G enius- that he had inspired, encouraged or enhanced. In the short time that he lived, you would have never considered the time he spent with the many he spent the time with.

Angela Winbush sang the first song, at the request of his father - Because Gerald had an infectious smile, she sang, YOUR SMILE. She looks good, and sounds even better.
That was followed by a montage of several of his spectaculars; it was illustrated at the cheers of the nearly packed Public Hall.

Men At Large sang the song that many people have played, someone sing, or request David Tolliver and Jason Champion sing when a loved one has been taken. "So Alone". That was the song that was written because of my sister - and while the song was in the process, Jason lost his father, and one of the writer's Edwin Tony Nicholas lost 'his' mother. The newest member of the group, Gemini joined in a gospel arrangement of the song. Many of the celebrities that came in support of Gerald, just had words to say, like Brian McKnight.

The Rude Boys, another Gerald Levert creation and production, sang their number 1 song, "Written All Over Your Face". It was four when the song was out originally, but the new five included Buddy Banks, Larry Marcus, Melvin (sorry don't remember his last name), Joe Little and Dwight Thompson. They were joined by Steve from the group TROOP.

Christopher Williams was there, Clifton Powell, "Pinky" from the ICE-CUBE/Friday series. He did his routine, because it was one of Gerald's favorite characters. The audience went crazy when he did the little routine that has become his benchmark. Bobby Brown was there, Tyler Perry and Keith Sweat. In fact, Keith Sweat joined Johnny Gill, as they performed "Baby I'm Ready". Johnny Gill is an electric performer. Through the hugs and the tears, we were in for one of the best salutations anyone can have in their honor.

The remaining members of Levert were acknowledged, his little brother Sean, and Marc Gordon. Ed Gordon was there to say a few words.

Gerald at the podium, Lynn Tolliver (center & in photo), Ralph Poole

photo by Michael Lilly

Gerald Levert
@ the Lynn Tolliver Roast
in Cleveland, Ohio

Kim Whitley and Yolanda Adams were each other's rock and strength. They had their words, and Ms Adams sang a piece of "That's What Friends Are For". Kelly Price was there, Usher.

A decent list of political players attended. Cleveland Mayor, Frank Jackson, which acknowledged a couple of streets being named after Gerald Levert and The O'jays who have been recently inducted into the Rock N Roll Hall of Fame, where they belong. I'm sure Gerald will have his place there, too.
The family members had their expressions, and brother Sean started the song, "Dance With My Father", with their father, Eddie.

One of the more dynamic speakers, was radio and BET star, Donnie Simpson.

Watching the sorrow - I couldn't keep from crying (which is not above me), but I told the audience that I was crying because I couldn't sing as well as some of the performers that had been on stage, but then later came back and said why I was crying.
The big star was Stevie Wonder, who sang with Eddie, also. And this note - Stevie Wonder flew coach and cancelled what he was doing, to get to Cleveland to help send Gerald Levert off.

Judge Mathis was there, but it was a court of a different matter. He said he wasn't a preacher, but went on to do a very soul stirring delivery that had everyone's heart in his hands, unlike the gavel he usually uses on TV in court.

One of the speakers said, it hurts now, but one day we will be able to hear the music of Gerald Levert and feel good and feel okay, like we do when we hear Marvin Gaye, or the Temptations, but I say to you - I won't. I didn't know Marvin Gaye, never met him. I didn't 'know' the Temptations - I didn't really know Barry White or Luther Vandross. Never had the chance to get acquainted with Rick James. I knew Gerald Levert. I played his first record, and you could say I was his radio father. Although I am ecstatic that he accomplished so much - I will never be happy that he is not here. EVER. I will repeat to you, what Eddie Levert said several times and it was repeated - LOVE YOURSELF and LOVE EACH OTHER. You will be amazed at the results you will see if you do.

Let me repeat, LOVE YOURSELF and LOVE EACH OTHER. If I left anyone's name out that performed, please accept my humble apology.

The following links will download the PDF files of the Gerald Levert Memorial program (thanks to Urban Insite & Kelly Macfor for the provision of these documents).

Gerald Levert Memorial Program
http://www.urbaninsite.com/gerald_memorial_prog.pdf

Gerald Levert Picture Tribute
http://www.urbaninsite.com/geraldlevertpictribute.pdf

In the beginning there was four,
and even though now there are more,
there are less for me...

This Dying Thing

..... you don't know how many times I cried while putting this together...... you just don't. There was sorrow, but also joy - having known my immediate family - really knowing them - hoping that this will help you through the grief of yours, inspired by my ma - I can remember my sister, she called me daily, my father/he spanked me, angrily at times, so I would do the right thing - My mother..I can hear her calling me now...and it hurts

Orrin, jr.